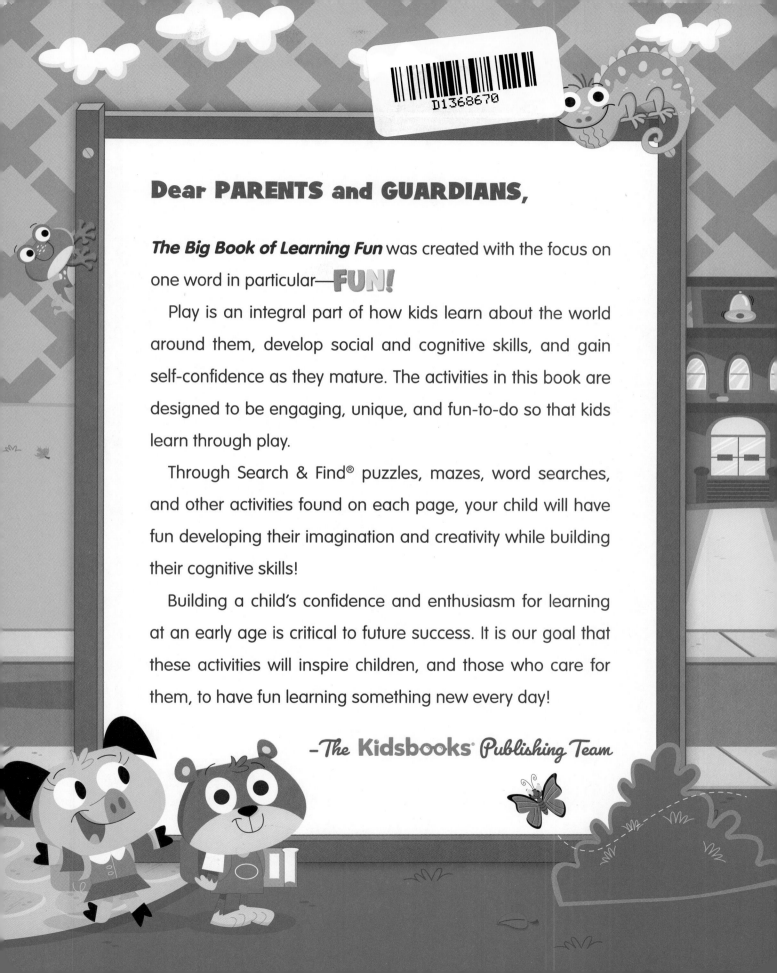

Dear PARENTS and GUARDIANS,

The Big Book of Learning Fun was created with the focus on one word in particular—**FUN!**

Play is an integral part of how kids learn about the world around them, develop social and cognitive skills, and gain self-confidence as they mature. The activities in this book are designed to be engaging, unique, and fun-to-do so that kids learn through play.

Through Search & Find® puzzles, mazes, word searches, and other activities found on each page, your child will have fun developing their imagination and creativity while building their cognitive skills!

Building a child's confidence and enthusiasm for learning at an early age is critical to future success. It is our goal that these activities will inspire children, and those who care for them, to have fun learning something new every day!

–The **Kidsbooks**® *Publishing Team*

Kidsbooks®

Kidsbooks Publishing
3535 West Peterson Avenue
Chicago, IL 60659
Printed in China
www.kidsbookspublishing.com

REBUS FUN

Solve the rebus puzzle to answer this question:

What do you do before a long car ride?

 - AN +  - P ___ ___ ___ ___

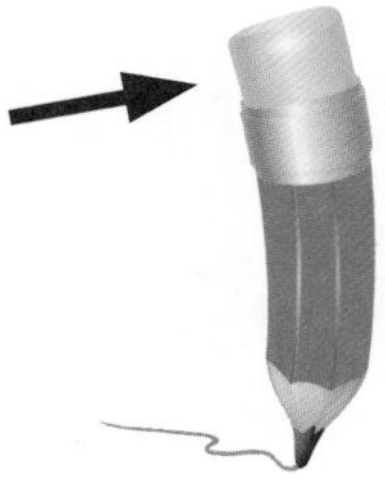 - ASER ' ___ ___

 - C ___ ___

Answer:

________ ' ________ ________

ANSWERS

REBUS FUN

Solve the rebus puzzle to answer this question:

What do you do before a long car ride?

 - AN +  - P F I L L

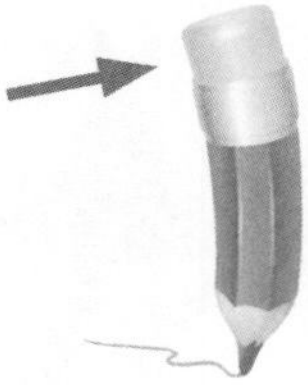 - ASER ’ E R

 - C U P

Answer:

FILL ’ ER UP

LET'S CIRCLE!

Circle five things that start with the letter **D**.

O
V
N
T

ANSWERS

LET'S CIRCLE!

Circle five things that start with the letter **D**.

O
V
N

LET'S FIND WORDS!

Look at the puzzle and see if you can find each word listed.
They are all things you use to build a snowman!
Look for the words across, up and down, and diagonally.

BUTTONS	HAT	SCARF
CARROT	PIPE	SNOW

S	Y	M	S	E	C	B
C	J	H	P	H	U	J
A	W	L	A	T	P	Y
R	P	I	T	T	I	E
F	T	O	M	R	P	C
S	N	O	W	O	E	J
S	C	A	R	R	O	T

ANSWERS

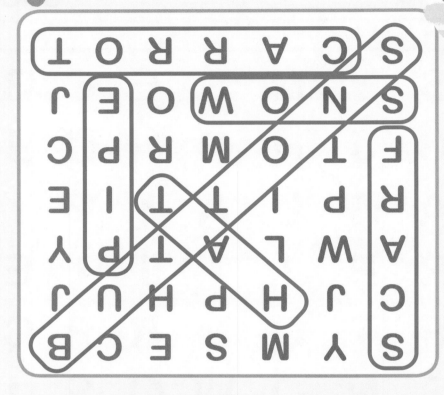

LET'S FIND WORDS!

Look at the puzzle and see if you can find each word listed.
They are all things you use to build a snowman!
Look for the words across, up and down, and diagonally.

BUTTONS	HAT	SCARF
CARROT	PIPE	SNOW

S	Y	M	S	E	C	B
C	J	H	P	H	U	J
A	W	L	A	T	P	Y
R	P	I	T	T	I	E
F	T	O	M	R	P	C
S	N	O	W	O	E	J
S	C	A	R	R	O	T

LOOK-ALIKES

Which two snowflakes are exactly the same?

ANSWERS

LOOK-ALIKES

Which two snowflakes are exactly the same?

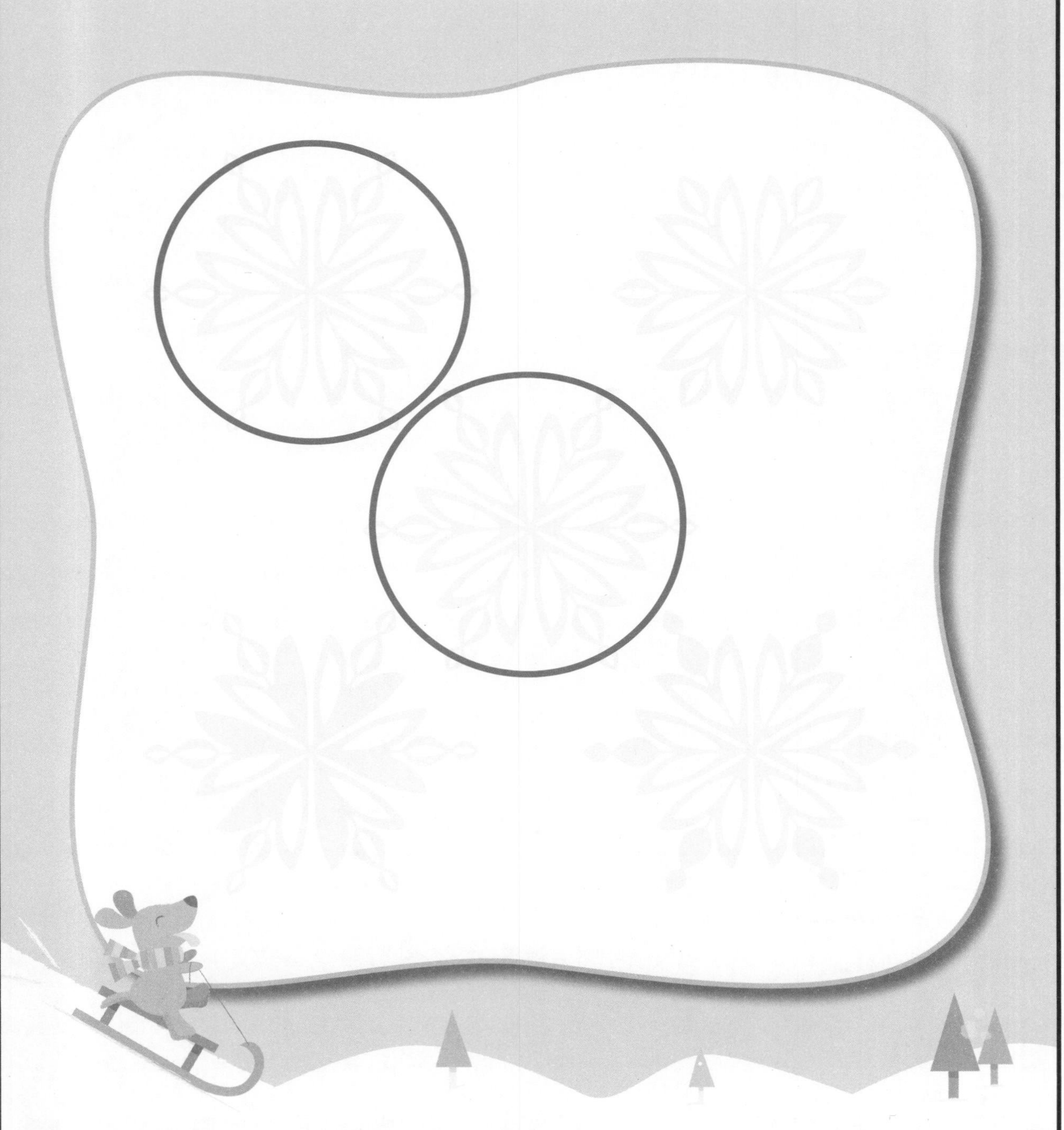

FIX 'N' MATCH

Unscramble the words on the left.
Then match the clothes that go together.

SUTI _____ ○

SOKCS _____ ○

STNAP _____ ○

AHT _____ ○

○

○

○

○

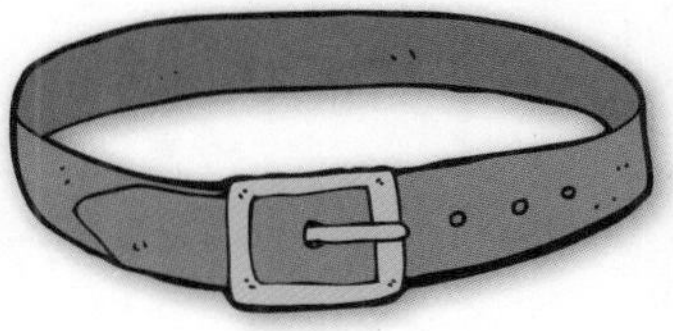

ANSWERS

FIX 'N' MATCH

Unscramble the words on the left.
Then match the clothes that go together.

SUTI SUIT

SOKCS SOCKS

STNAP PANTS

AHT HAT

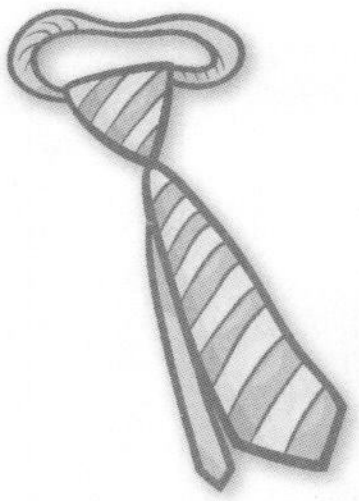

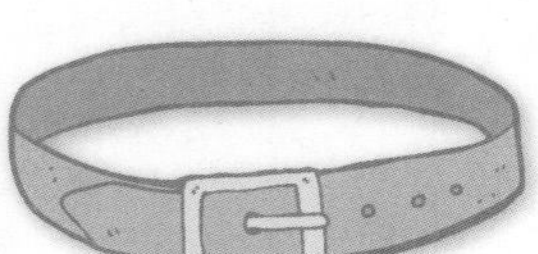

MAZE CRAZE SEASHELLS!

Help collect seashells to go in the pail.
The correct path is made up of only shells.
You may not move diagonally.

START

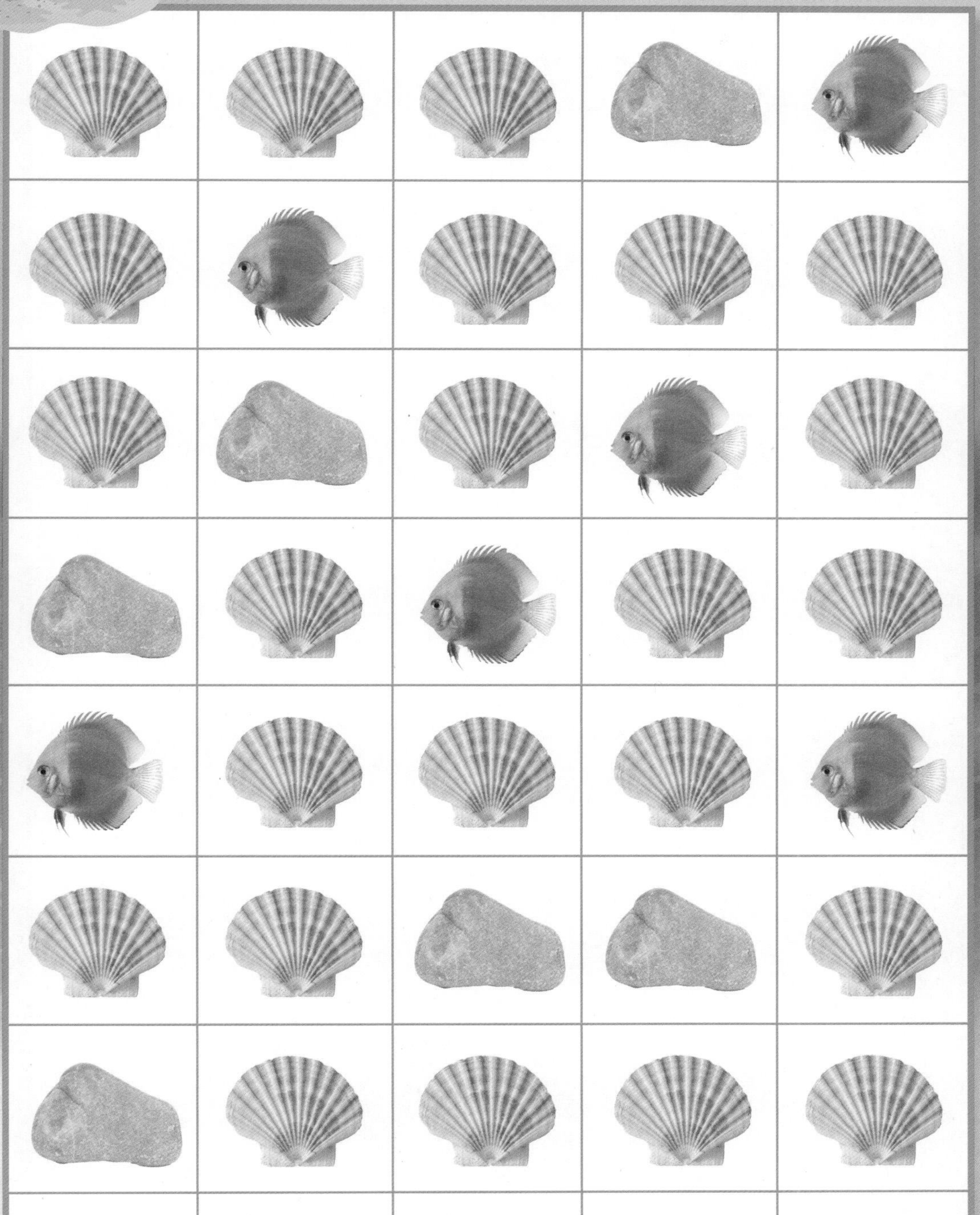

FINISH

ANSWERS

MAZE CRAZE SEASHELLS!

Help collect seashells to go in the pail.
The correct path is made up of only shells.
You may not move diagonally.

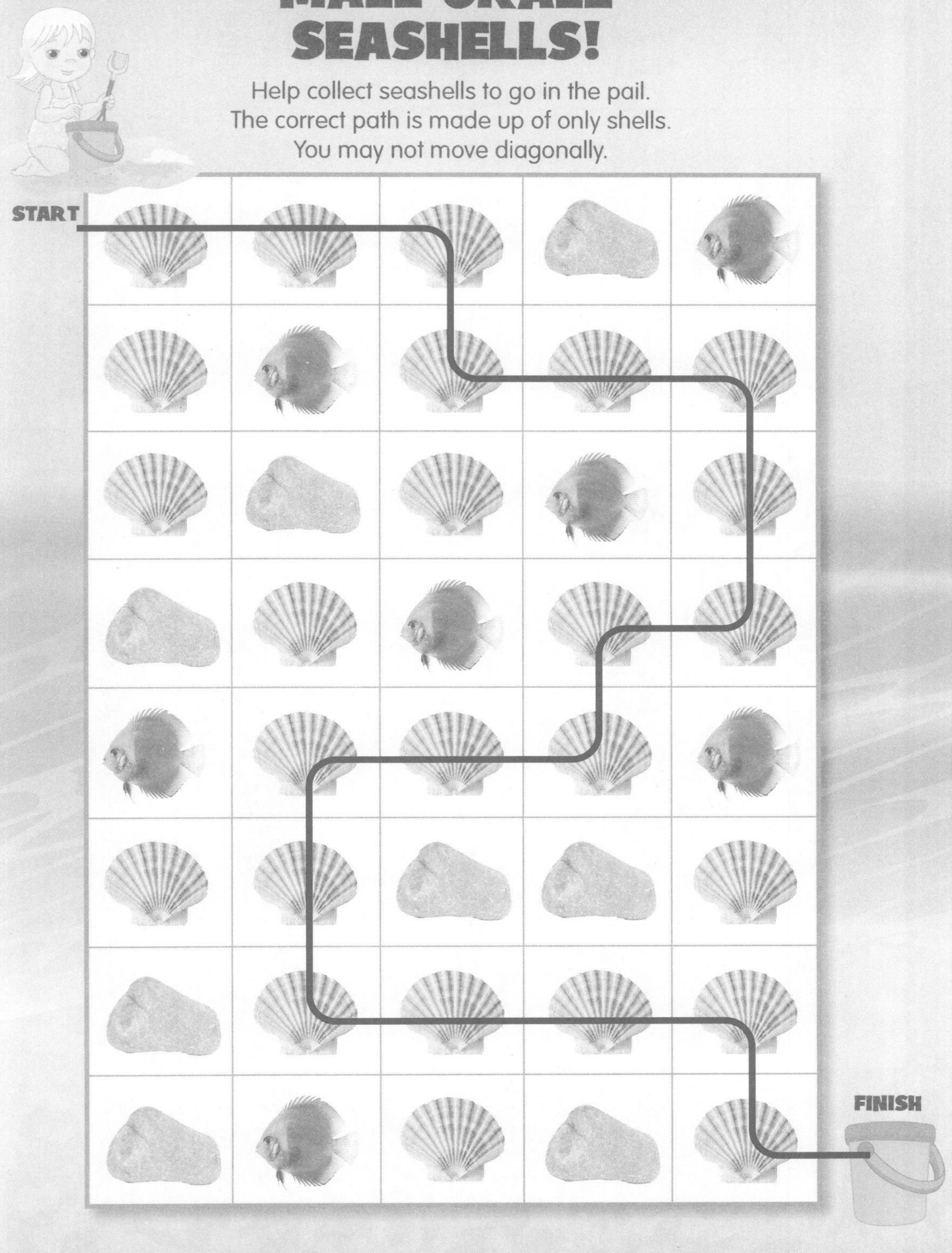
START
FINISH

SPOT THE DIFFERENCE AT THE AIR SHOW

Circle five things that are different in these two pictures.

AIR SHOW

AIR SHOW

ANSWERS

SPOT THE DIFFERENCE AT THE AIR SHOW

Circle five things that are different in these two pictures.

AIR SHOW

AIR SHOW

LOOK-ALIKES

Which two pictures are exactly the same?

ANSWERS

LOOK-ALIKES

Which two pictures are exactly the same?

LET'S MAKE WORDS!

Write as many words as you can that start with the letter **V**.
Be creative! See if you can think of five words.

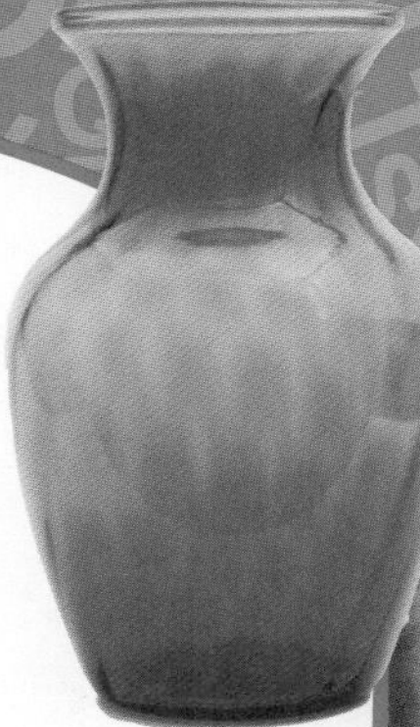

V ______________________

V ______________________

V ______________________

V ______________________

V ______________________

ANSWERS

LET'S MAKE WORDS!

Write as many words as you can that start with the letter **V**.
Be creative! See if you can think of five words.

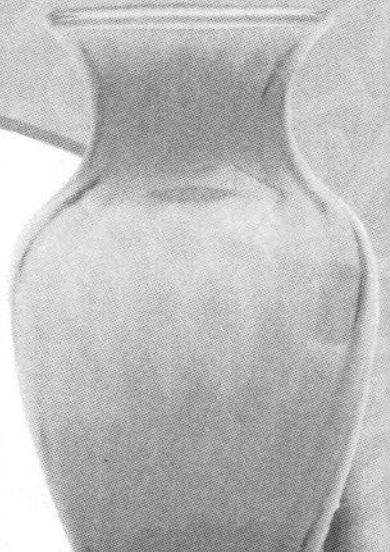

Here are a few words:

VIOLIN

VALENTINE

VASE

VIDEO

VINE

DOT TO DOT

Who is walking the tightrope at the circus?
Connect the dots from 1 to 35 and find out!

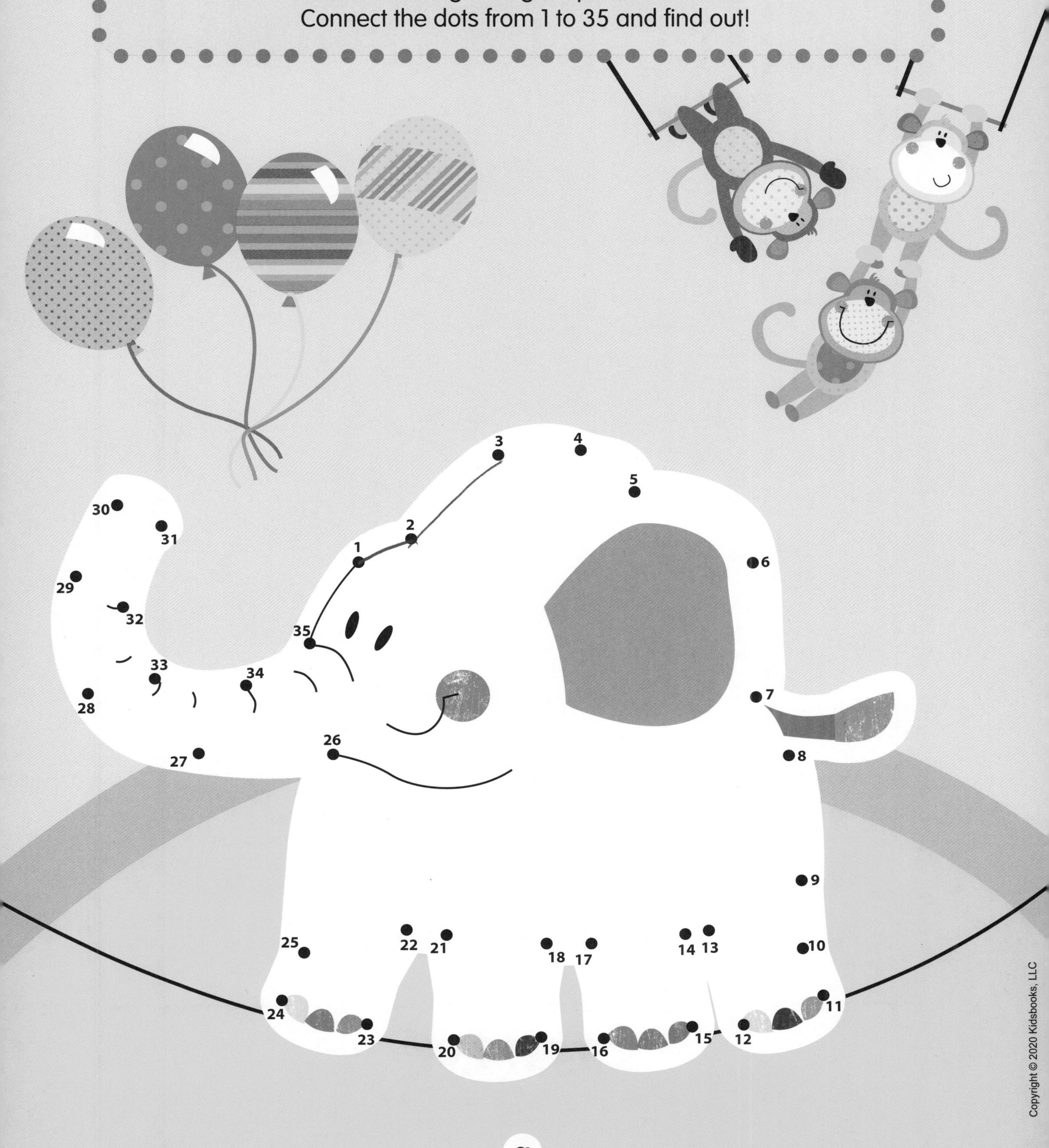

ANSWERS

DOT TO DOT

Who is walking the tightrope at the circus?
Connect the dots from 1 to 35 and find out!

LET'S CIRCLE!

Circle five things that start with the letter **L**.

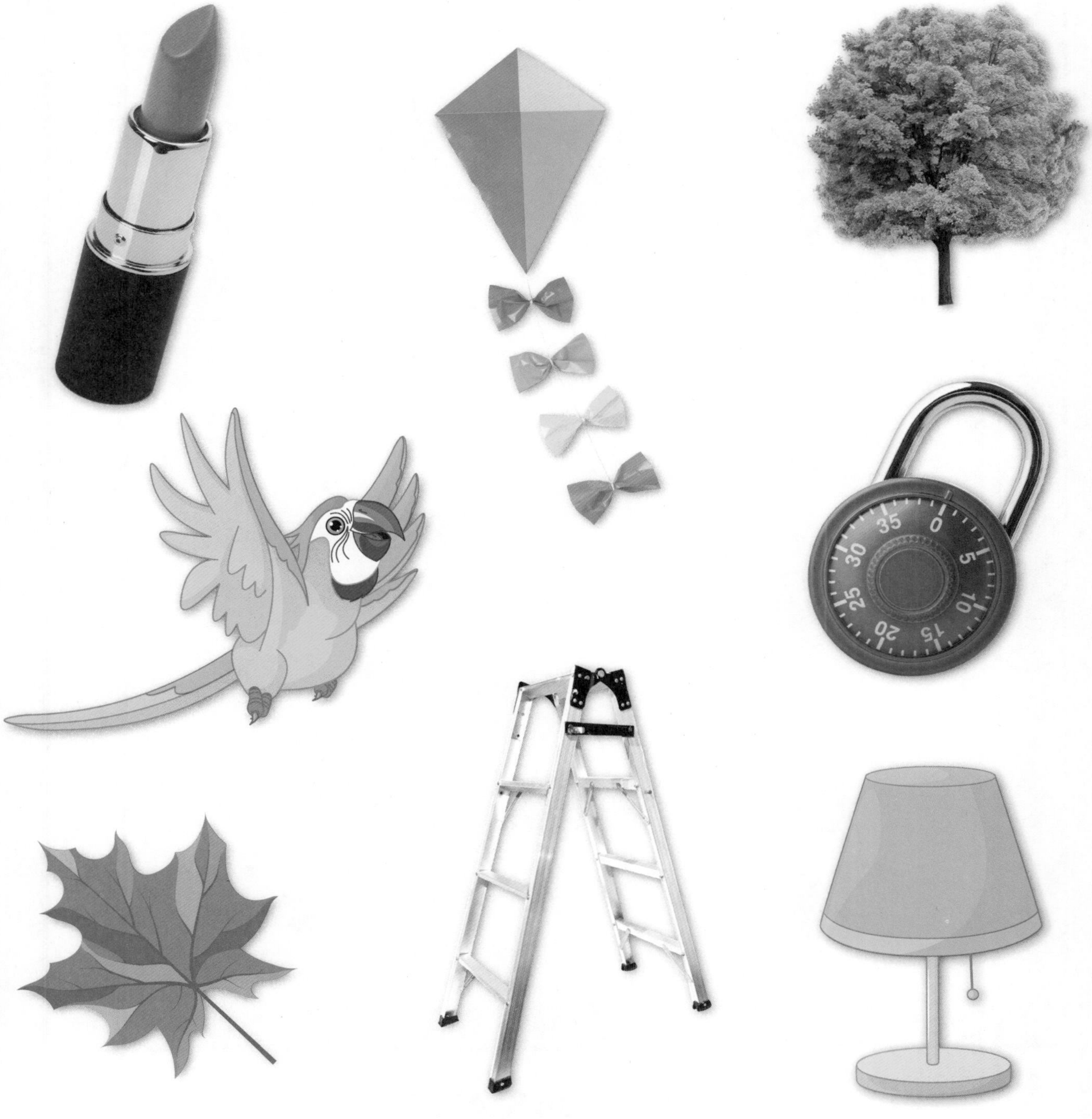

35
0
30
5
25
10
20
15

ANSWERS

LET'S CIRCLE!

Circle five things that start with the letter **L**.

SECRET CODE

Shh! Use the secret code to answer the riddle:

What did the right eye say to the left eye?

1=M	3=I	5=N	7=G	9=E
2=H	4=L	6=O	8=S	10=T

Answer:
BETWEEN YOU AND ME,

___ ___ ___ ___ ___ ___ ___ ___ ___

8 6 1 9 10 2 3 5 7

___ ___ ___ ___ ___ ___

8 1 9 4 4 8

ANSWERS

SECRET CODE

Shh! Use the secret code to answer the riddle:

What did the right eye say to the left eye?

1=M	3=I	5=N	7=G	9=E
2=H	4=L	6=O	8=S	10=T

Answer:
BETWEEN YOU AND ME,

S	O	M	E	T	H	I	N	G
8	6	1	9	10	2	3	5	7

S	M	E	L	L	S
8	1	9	4	4	8

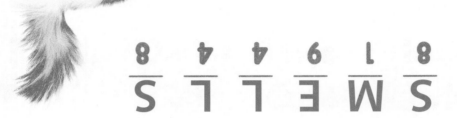

SHOP AND SPEND!

Pam has $20. Help her spend it all! What three items should she buy for exactly that amount?

Book
$8

Socks
$5

Poster
$9

Hoodie
$19

Shorts
$16

Hat
$7

ANSWERS

SHOP AND SPEND!

Pam has $20. Help her spend it all! What three items should she buy for exactly that amount?

Book
$8
Socks
$5
Poster
$9
Hoodie
$19
Shorts
$16
Hat
$7

NAME THE SPORT

Look at each ball and write the name of the sport it is used for to complete the crossword puzzle.

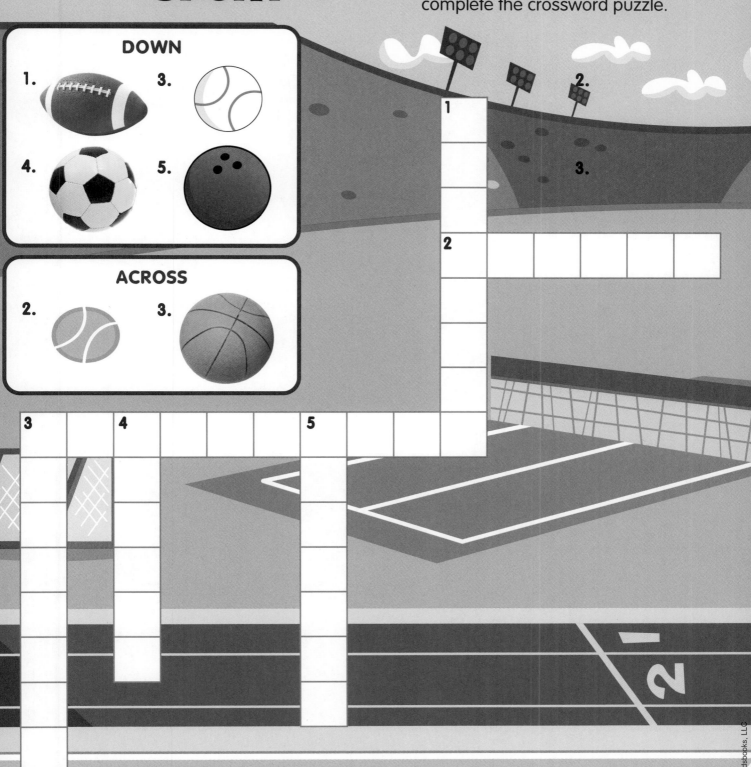

DOWN

1. 

3. 

4. 

5. 

ACROSS

2. 

3. 

ANSWERS

NAME THE SPORT

Look at each ball and write the name of the sport it is used for to complete the crossword puzzle.

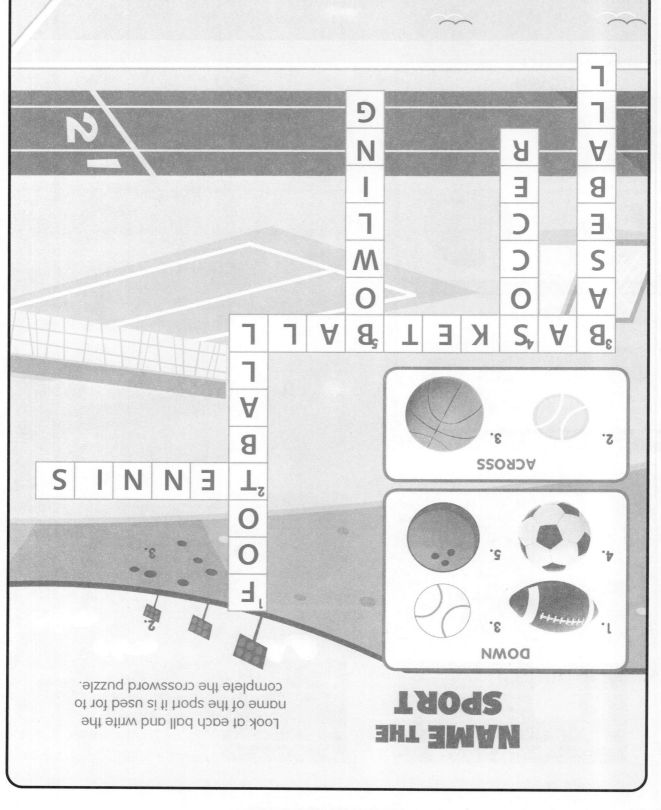

DOWN
1.
3.
4.
5.
ACROSS
2.
3.
FOOTBALL
TENNIS
BASKETBALL
BASEBALL
SOCCER
BOWLING

REBUS FUN

Solve the rebus puzzle to answer this question:

Who was the first astronaut to walk on the moon?

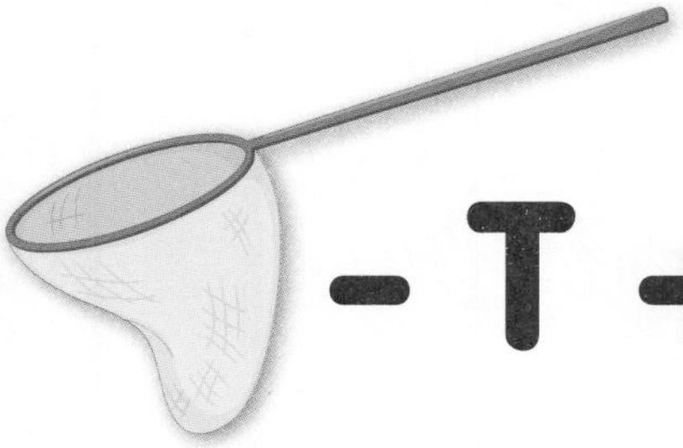 - T + 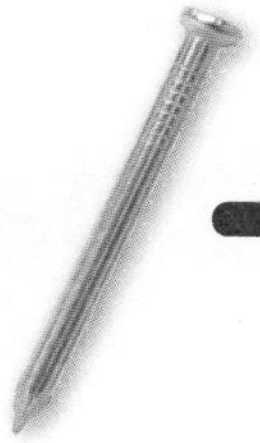 - NA ___ ___ ___ ___

 +  - ING +  - E

\+  - HOST

___ ___ ___ ___ ___ ___ ___ ___ ___

Answer:

________________ ________________________

ANSWERS

REBUS FUN

Solve the rebus puzzle to answer this question:

Who was the first astronaut to walk on the moon?

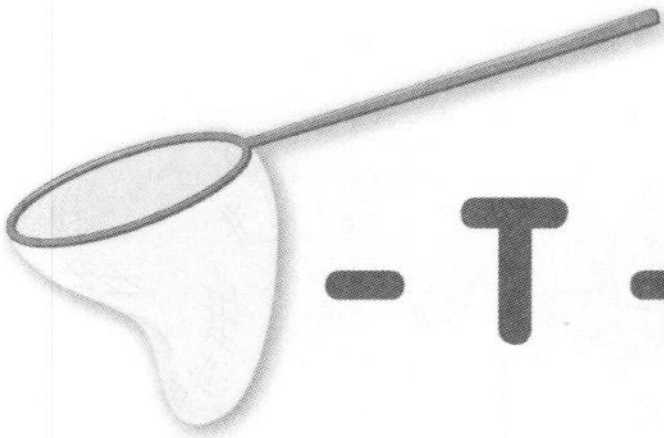 - T + 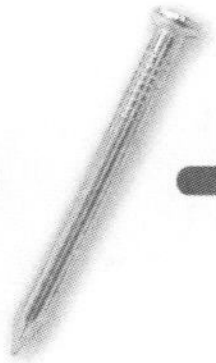 - NA N E I L

 +  - ING + 1 - E

+  - HOST

A R M S T R O N G

Answer:

NEIL ARMSTRONG

LET'S CIRCLE!

Circle five things that start with the letter **T**.

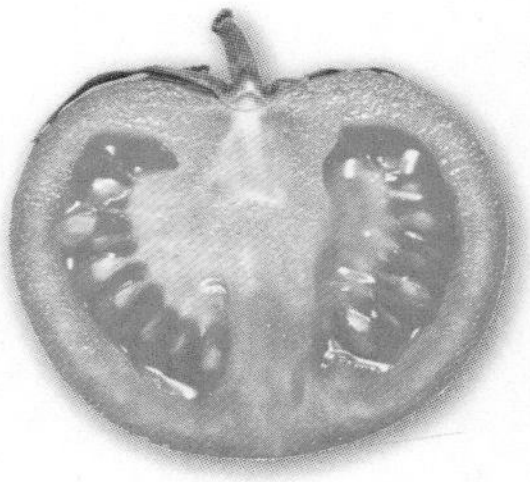

SCHOOL BUS
STOP
SCHOOL BUS

ANSWERS

LET'S CIRCLE!

Circle five things that start with the letter **T**.

SCHOOL BUS
STOP
SCHOOL BUS

RIDDLE TIME!

Write the first letter of each object to answer this riddle:

Why was the math book sad?

_____ _____ _____ _____

_____ _____ _____ _____

Answer:

IT HAD ______________________________

ANSWERS

RIDDLE TIME!

Write the first letter of each object to answer this riddle:

Why was the math book sad?

P

R

O

B

L

E

M

S

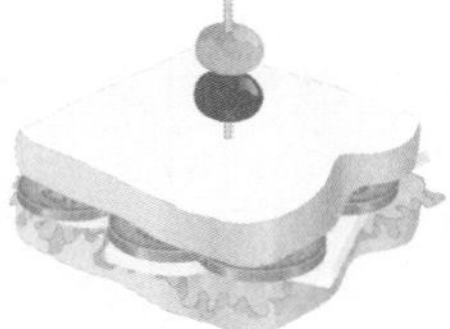

Answer:

IT HAD PROBLEMS

FIX 'N' MATCH

Unscramble the words on the left.
Then match the things that rhyme.

AMPL _____ ○

TAC _____ ○

PALI _____ ○

SHID _____ ○

SEHOU _____ ○

MOUSE

STAMP

BAT

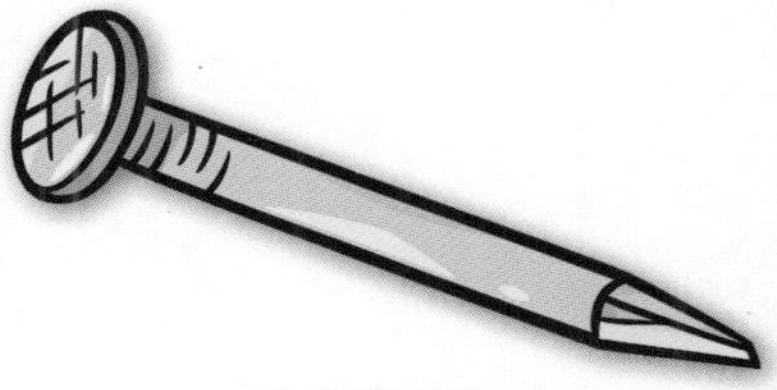

NAIL

FISH

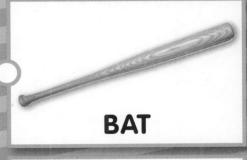

ANSWERS

FIX 'N' MATCH

Unscramble the words on the left.
Then match the things that rhyme.

AMPL LAMP

TAC CAT

PALI PAIL

SHID DISH

SEHOU HOUSE

MOUSE

STAMP

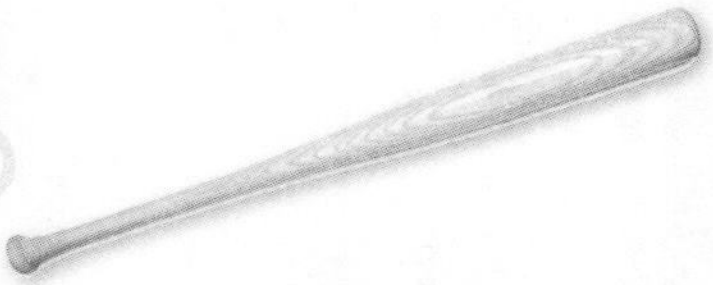

BAT

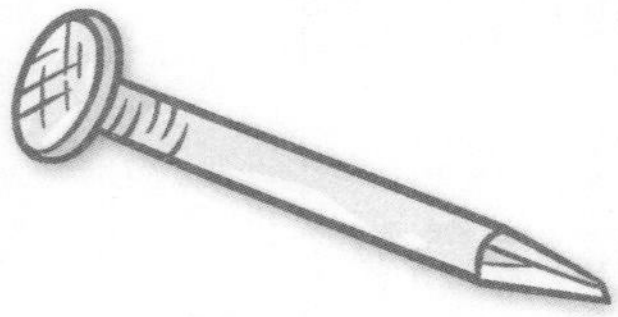

NAIL

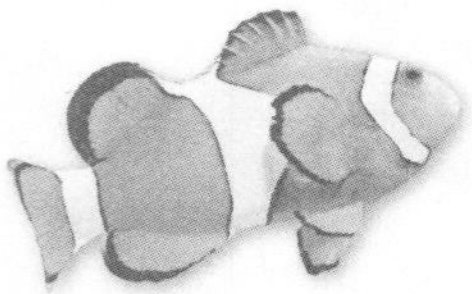

FISH

LET'S FIND WORDS!

Look at the puzzle and see if you can find each word listed. They all start with the letter **W**! Look for the words across and up and down.

WHEEL

WAFFLE

WATCH

WINDOW

WORM

WALRUS

R	W	K	J	L	G	S	I	O	R
S	H	G	E	D	E	O	R	W	A
C	E	P	W	A	T	C	H	I	H
L	E	O	U	H	A	E	B	N	R
E	L	T	C	F	V	E	E	D	E
W	A	L	R	U	S	E	L	O	N
F	A	N	M	L	B	D	L	W	W
W	A	F	F	L	E	E	P	V	O
C	R	Q	C	P	O	D	A	N	R
W	O	E	G	G	W	U	R	H	M

ANSWERS

LET'S FIND WORDS!

Look at the puzzle and see if you can find each word listed. They all start with the letter **W**! Look for the words across and up and down.

WHEEL

WAFFLE

WATCH

WORM

WALRUS

WINDOW

R	W	K	J	L	G	S	I	O	R
S	H	G	E	D	E	O	R	W	A
C	E	P	W	A	T	C	H	I	H
L	E	O	U	H	A	E	B	N	R
E	L	T	C	F	V	E	E	D	E
W	A	L	R	U	S	E	L	O	N
F	A	N	M	L	B	D	L	W	W
W	A	F	F	L	E	E	P	V	O
C	R	Q	C	P	O	D	A	N	R
W	O	E	G	G	W	U	R	H	M

MAZE CRAZE PENGUINS!

Help this penguin find its two friends.
Count by 2s from 2 to 44 to follow the correct path.
You may not move diagonally.

START

2	1	10	12	14
4	6	8	17	16
7	5	3	20	18
29	26	24	22	27
30	28	31	37	33
32	34	36	38	35
41	43	39	40	42
45	51	47	53	44

FINISH

ANSWERS

MAZE CRAZE PENGUINS!

Help this penguin find its two friends.
Count by 2s from 2 to 44 to follow the correct path.
You may not move diagonally.

START

2	1	10	12	14
4	6	8	17	16
7	5	3	20	18
29	26	24	22	27
30	28	31	37	33
32	34	36	38	35
41	43	39	40	42
45	51	47	53	44

FINISH

LET'S MAKE WORDS!

Write as many words as you can that start with the letter **C**.
Be creative! See if you can think of five words.

C ______________________

C ______________________

C ______________________

C ______________________

C ______________________

ANSWERS

LET'S MAKE WORDS!

Write as many words as you can that start with the letter **C**.
Be creative! See if you can think of five words.

Here are a few words:

CAT

CUPCAKES

CAR

CARROT

CUP

CAN YOU FIND?

Search, find, and circle these things at the beach!

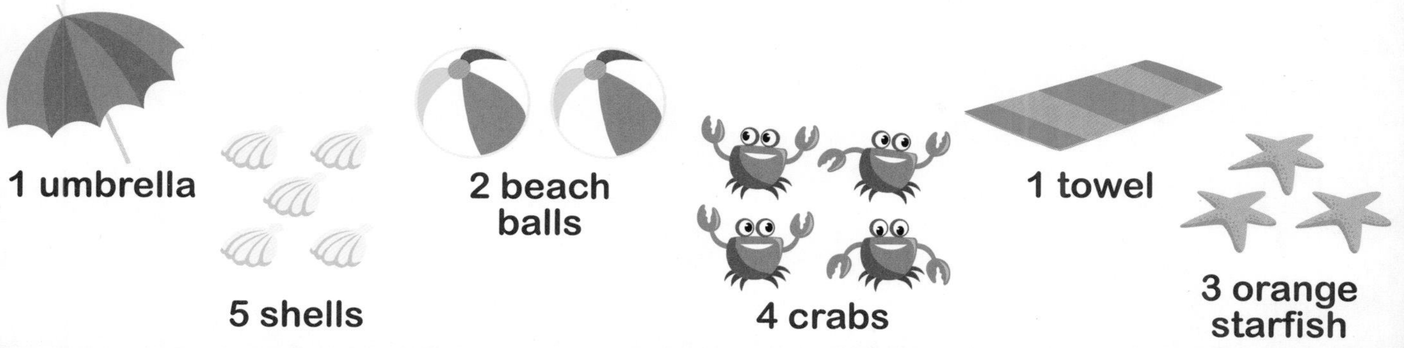
1 umbrella
5 shells
2 beach balls
4 crabs
1 towel
3 orange starfish

ANSWERS

CAN YOU FIND?

Search, find, and circle these things at the beach!

1 umbrella

5 shells

2 beach balls

4 crabs

1 towel

3 orange starfish

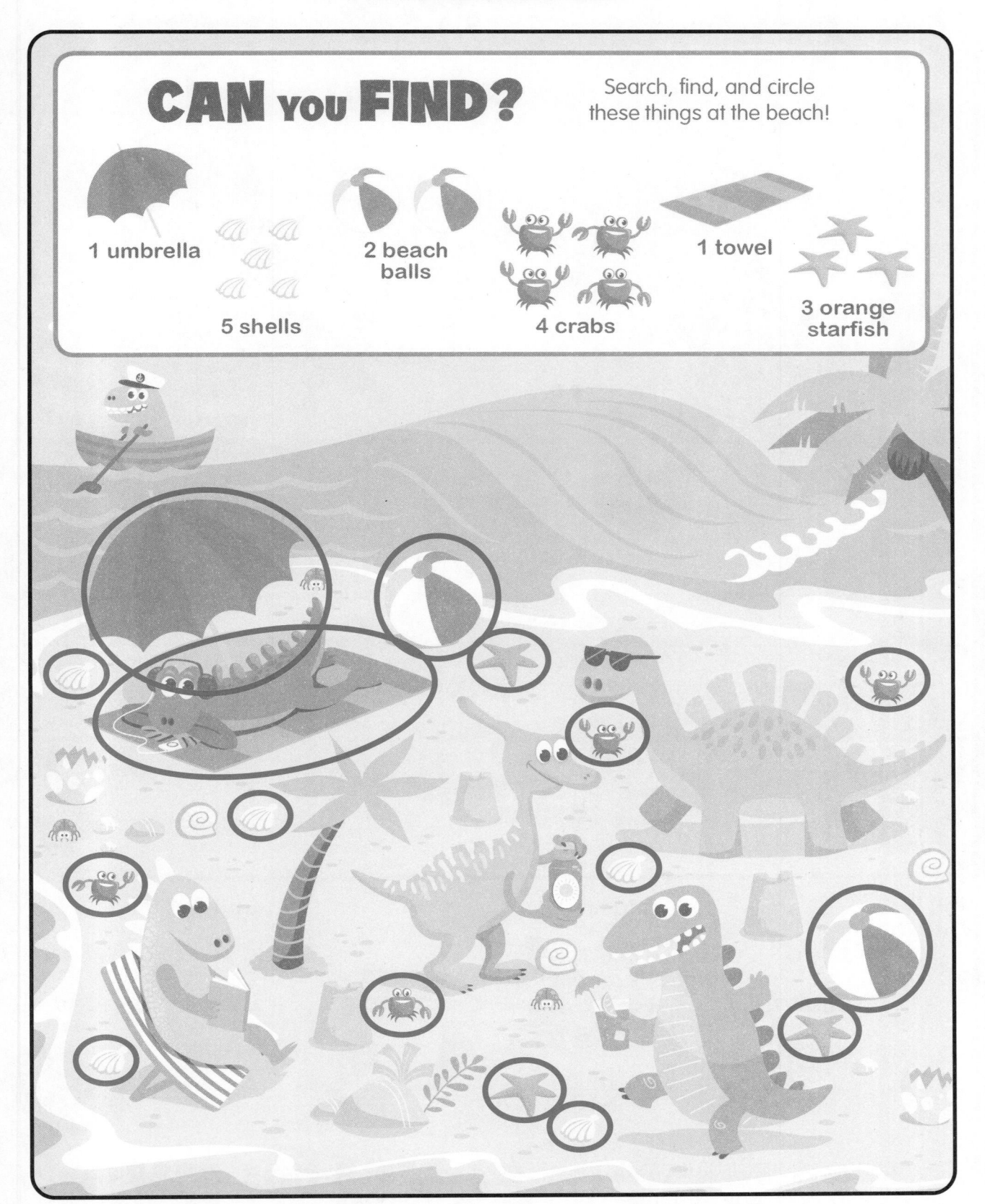

DOT TO DOT

What's this hamster's favorite part of the playground?
Connect the dots from 1 to 25 and find out!

1
2
3
4
5
6
7
8
9
10
11
12
13
14
15
16
17
18
19
20
21
22
23
24
25

ANSWERS

DOT to DOT

What's this hamster's favorite part of the playground?
Connect the dots from 1 to 25 and find out!

1
2
3
4
5
6
7
8
9
10
11
12
13
14
15
16
17
18
19
20
21
22
23
24
25

NAME THE FARM ANIMALS

Use the picture clues to complete this crossword puzzle.

ACROSS

4. 

5. 

DOWN

1. 

2. 

3. 

1
2
3
4
5

ANSWERS

NAME THE FARM ANIMALS

Use the picture clues to complete this crossword puzzle.

ACROSS
4.
5.
DOWN
1.
2.
3.

1 HORSE
2 COW
3 HEN
4 ROOSTER
5 SHEEP

FILL IN THE BLANKS

Use the picture clues to fill in the missing letters.
Then write those letters in the space below to answer this question:

What is the fastest land animal?

__ __ AIR

B __ __ HIVE

1860-1861 PONY EXPRESS
UNITED STATES POSTAGE
4c

S __ __ MP

__ AMMER

Answer: **THE** ______________________________

ANSWERS

FILL IN THE BLANKS

Use the picture clues to fill in the missing letters.
Then write those letters in the space below to answer this question:

What is the fastest land animal?

C H A I R

B E E H I V E

4c
UNITED STATES POSTAGE
1860 1961 PONY EXPRESS

S T A M P

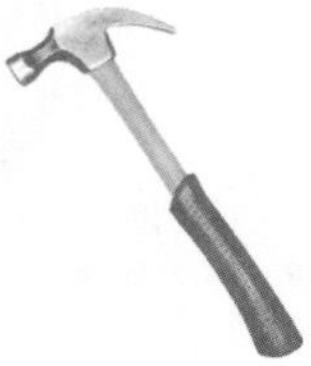

H A M M E R

Answer: **THE** CHEETAH

WHAT DOESN'T BELONG?

Circle one thing you would **NOT** find in a firehouse.

Fire Chief
FIRE CHIEF
FIREFIGHTER

ANSWERS

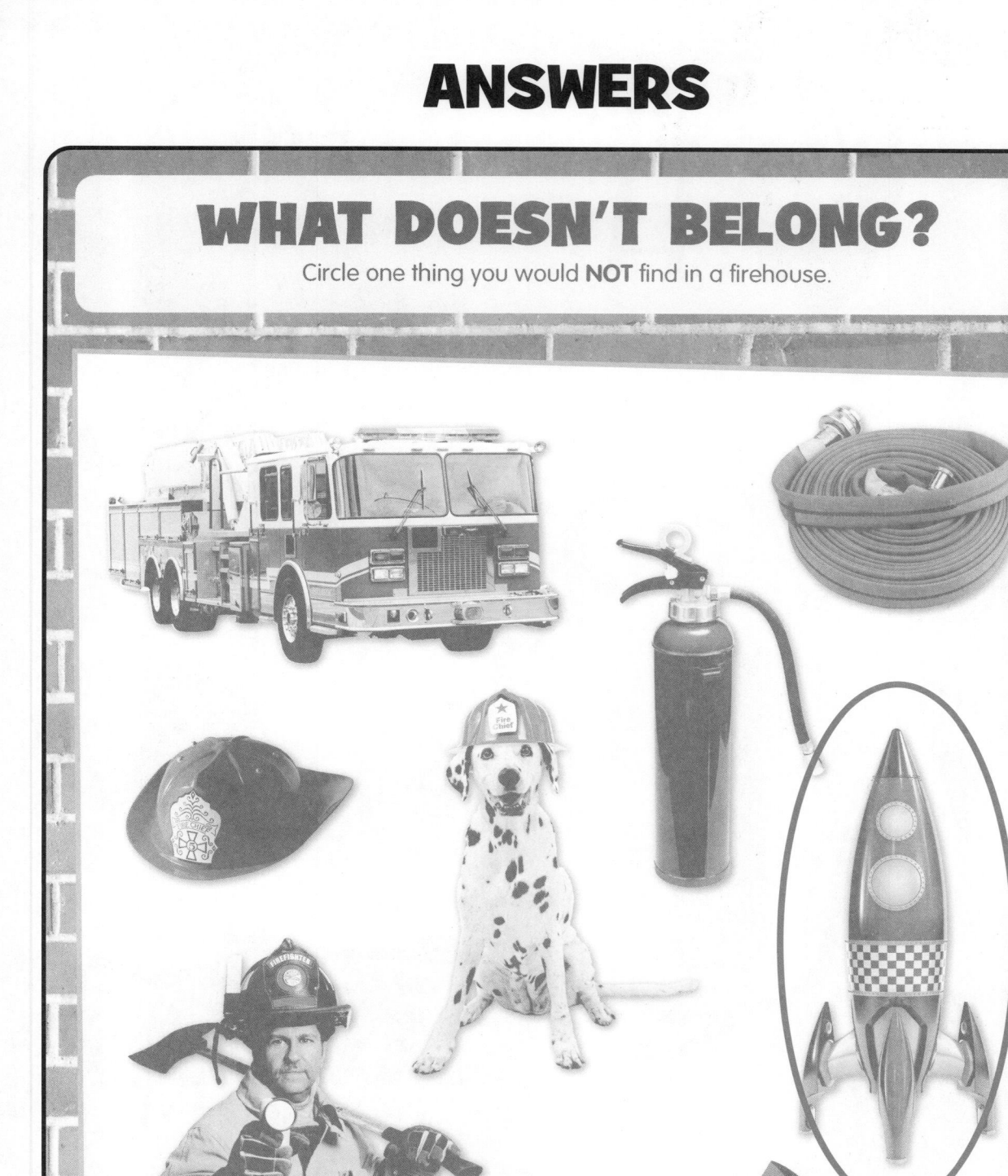

WHAT DOESN'T BELONG?

Circle one thing you would **NOT** find in a firehouse.

Fire Chief
FIREFIGHTER

DALMATIAN TWINS

Draw a line to connect each Dalmatian on the left to its exact twin on the right.

ANSWERS

DALMATIAN TWINS

Draw a line to connect each Dalmatian on the left to its exact twin on the right.

WHICH IS DIFFERENT?

Find one fire truck that is different from the rest.

23
23

23
23

23
23

23
23

23
23

ANSWERS

WHICH IS DIFFERENT?

Find one fire truck that is different from the rest.

CAN YOU FIND? Search, find, and circle seven things that are blue.

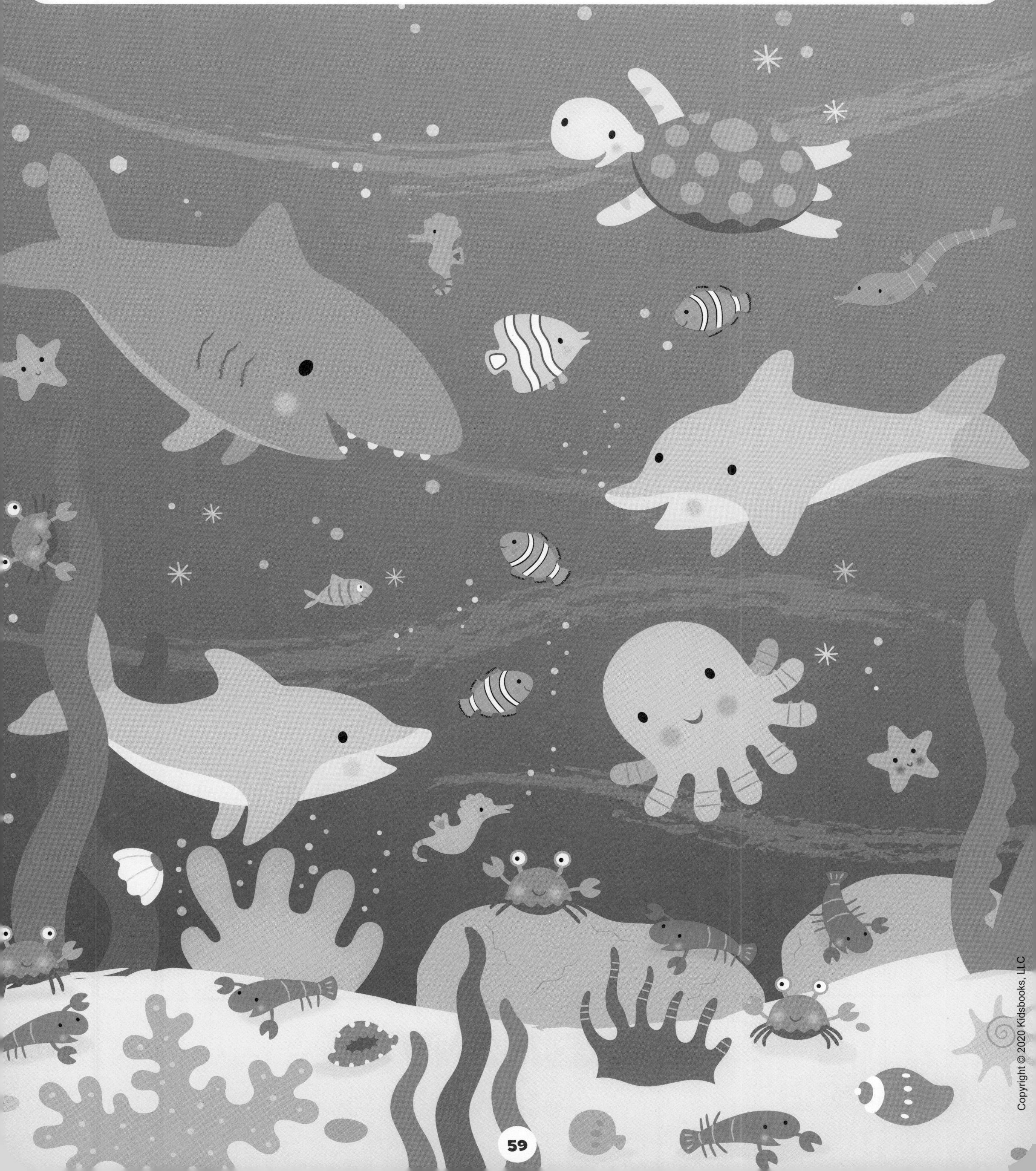

ANSWERS

CAN YOU FIND? Search, find, and circle seven things that are blue.

LET'S CIRCLE!

Circle five things that start with the letter **H**.

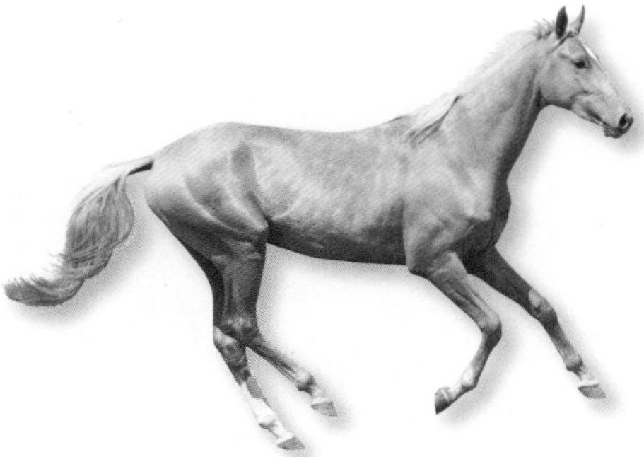

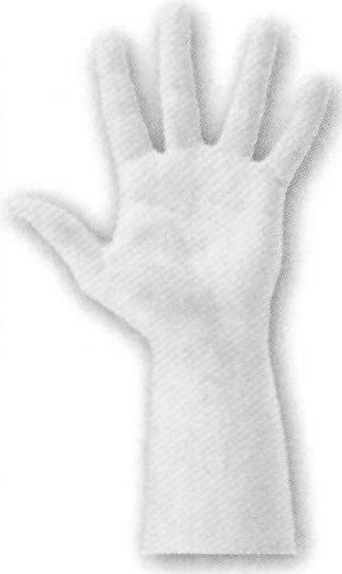

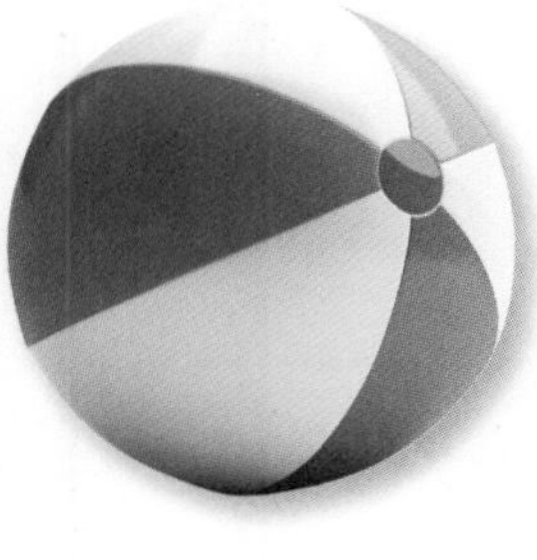

ANSWERS

LET'S CIRCLE!

Circle five things that start with the letter **H**.

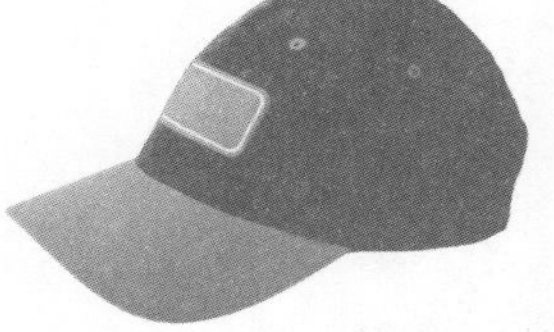

SECRET CODE

Shh! Use this secret code to answer this riddle:

What do you call a bear without any teeth?

1=B	3=M	5=R	7=G
2=U	4=A	6=Y	8=E

Answer:

___   ___ ___ ___ ___ ___

4   7 2 3 3 6

___ ___ ___ ___

1 8 4 5

ANSWERS

SECRET CODE

Shh! Use this secret code to answer this riddle:

What do you call a bear without any teeth?

1=B 3=M 5=R 7=G
2=U 4=A 6=Y 8=E

Answer:

A		G	U	M	M	Y
4		7	2	3	3	6

B	E	A	R
1	8	4	5

SPOT THE DIFFERENCE ON THE CAROUSEL

Circle five things that are different in these two pictures.

TICKETS

TICKETS

ANSWERS

SPOT THE DIFFERENCE ON THE CAROUSEL

Circle five things that are different in these two pictures.

TICKETS

TICKETS

LET'S FIND WORDS!

Look at the puzzle and see if you can
find each word listed. They are all desserts!
Look for the words across, up and down, and diagonally.

SWEET SHOP

BROWNIE	COOKIES	PIE
CAKE	FRUIT	PUDDING

C	Z	B	R	P	T	Y
F	O	R	E	U	I	I
R	A	O	G	D	S	C
U	W	W	K	D	R	A
I	K	N	P	I	E	K
T	S	I	X	N	E	E
Q	T	E	C	G	M	S

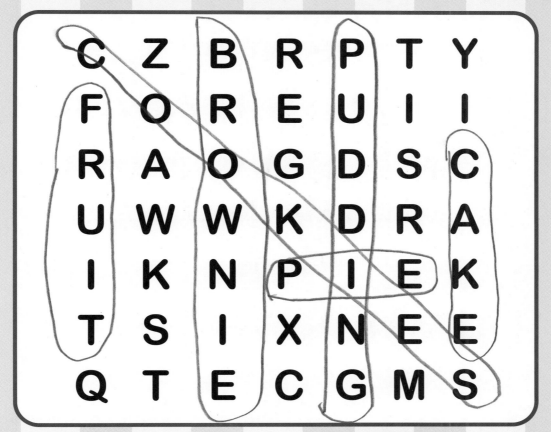

ANSWERS

LET'S FIND WORDS!

Look at the puzzle and see if you can find each word listed. They are all desserts! Look for the words across, up and down, and diagonally.

SWEET SHOP

BROWNIE	COOKIES	PIE
CAKE	FRUIT	PUDDING

C	Z	B	R	P	T	Y
F	O	R	E	U	I	I
R	A	O	G	D	S	C
U	W	W	K	D	R	A
I	K	N	P	I	E	K
T	S	I	X	N	E	E
Q	T	E	C	G	M	S

WHICH IS DIFFERENT?

Find one house that is different from the rest.

ANSWERS

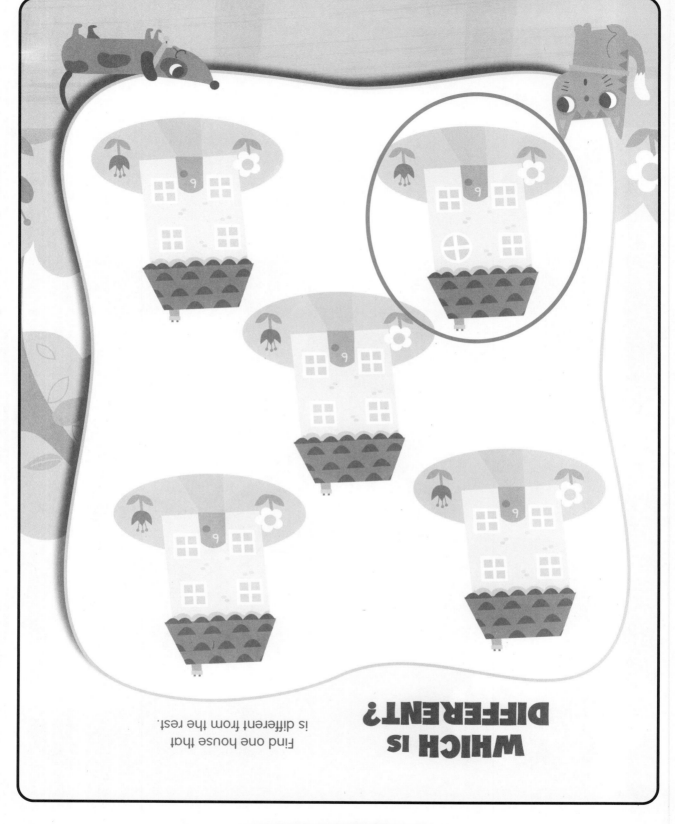

WHICH IS DIFFERENT?

Find one house that is different from the rest.

NAME IT AT THE LIBRARY

Use the picture clues to complete this crossword puzzle. They are all things you find at the library.

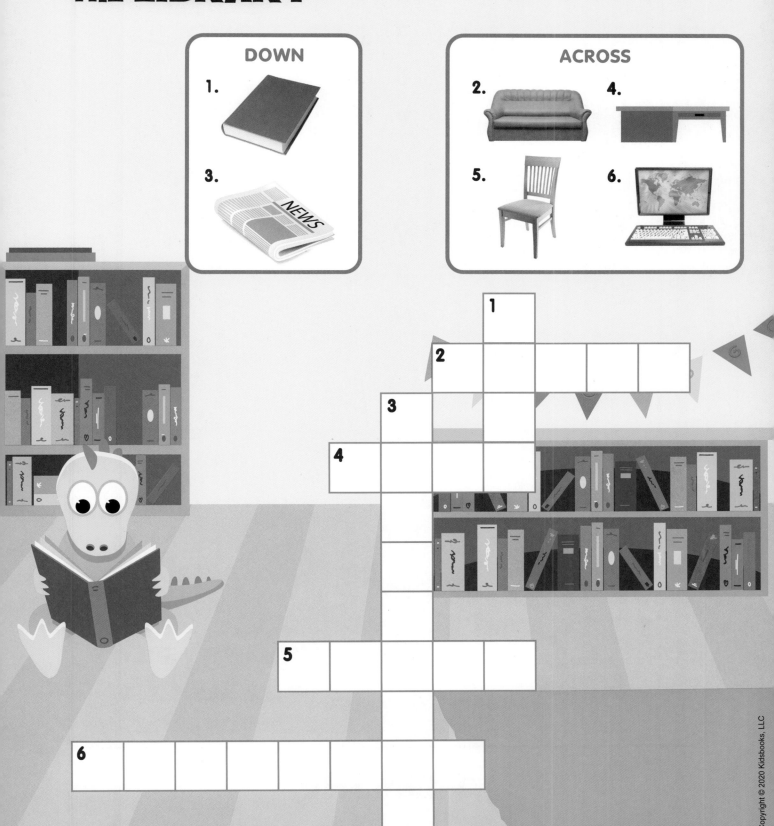

DOWN

1.

3.

NEWS

ACROSS

2.

4.

5.

6.

1
2
3
4
5
6

ANSWERS

NAME IT AT THE LIBRARY

Use the picture clues to complete this crossword puzzle. They are all things you find at the library.

DOWN

1. 

3. 
NEWS

ACROSS

2. 

4. 

5. 

6. 

1 BOOK
2 COUCH
3 NEWSPAPER
4 DESK
5 CHAIR
6 COMPUTER

LET'S MAKE WORDS!

Write as many words as you can that start with the letter **R**.
Be creative! See if you can think of five words.

R ____________________

R ____________________

R ____________________

R ____________________

R ____________________

ANSWERS

LET'S MAKE WORDS!

Write as many words as you can that start with the letter **R**.
Be creative! See if you can think of five words.

Here are a few words:

RABBIT

RUN

RATTLE

RACE

REST

REBUS FUN

Solve the rebus puzzle to answer this question:

What is the biggest ocean in the world?

 - BACK - K + 

- G - T + 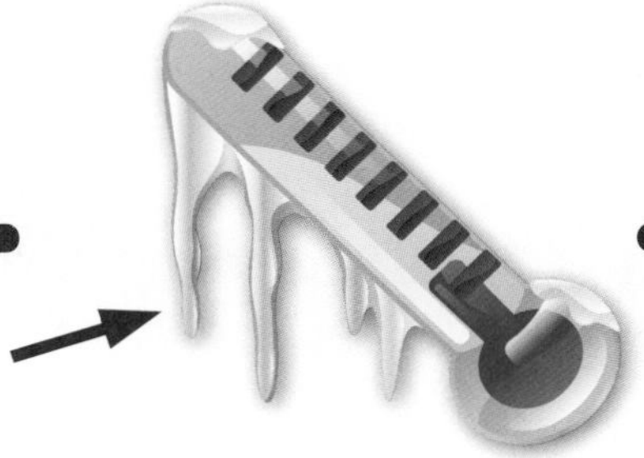 - ICLE

___ ___ ___ ___ ___ ___ ___

Answer:

THE ____________________ **OCEAN**

ANSWERS

REBUS FUN

Solve the rebus puzzle to answer this question:

What is the biggest ocean in the world?

 - BACK - K + 

- G - T + 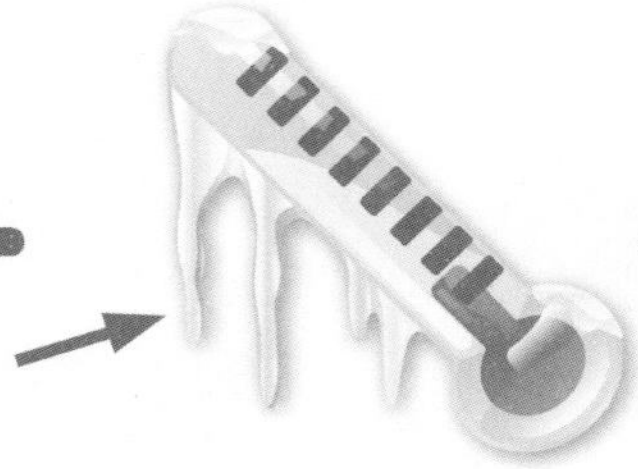 - ICLE

P A C I F I C

Answer:

THE PACIFIC OCEAN

MAZE CRAZE FLAMINGOS!

Help this flamingo find its friends to make a group of five.
Count by 5s from 5 to 100 to follow the correct path.
You may not move diagonally.

START

5	4	3	8	9
10	15	20	1	12
7	6	25	30	35
14	2	3	9	40
12	60	55	50	45
70	65	7	2	16
75	80	85	90	95
3	17	8	9	100

FINISH

ANSWERS

MAZE CRAZE FLAMINGOS!

Help this flamingo find its friends to make a group of five.
Count by 5s from 5 to 100 to follow the correct path.
You may not move diagonally.

START

5	4	3	8	9
10	15	20	1	12
7	6	25	30	35
14	2	3	9	40
12	60	55	50	45
70	65	7	2	16
75	80	85	90	95
3	17	8	9	100

FINISH

WHAT DOES IT SAY?

Unscramble these street signs to find out!

POTS

_ _ _ _

DAED NED

_ _ _ _ _   _ _ _

ENO AYW

_ _ _   _ _ _

OD TON NETER

_ _   _ _ _

_ _ _ _ _

IELDY

_ _ _ _ _

ANSWERS

WHAT DOES IT SAY?
Unscramble these street signs to find out!
POTS
STOP
DAED NED
DEAD END
ENO AYW
ONE WAY
OD TON NETER
DO NOT ENTER
IELDY
YIELD

TOUCAN TWINS

Draw a line to connect each toucan on the left to its exact twin on the right!

ANSWERS

TOUCAN TWINS

Draw a line to connect each toucan on the left to its exact twin on the right!

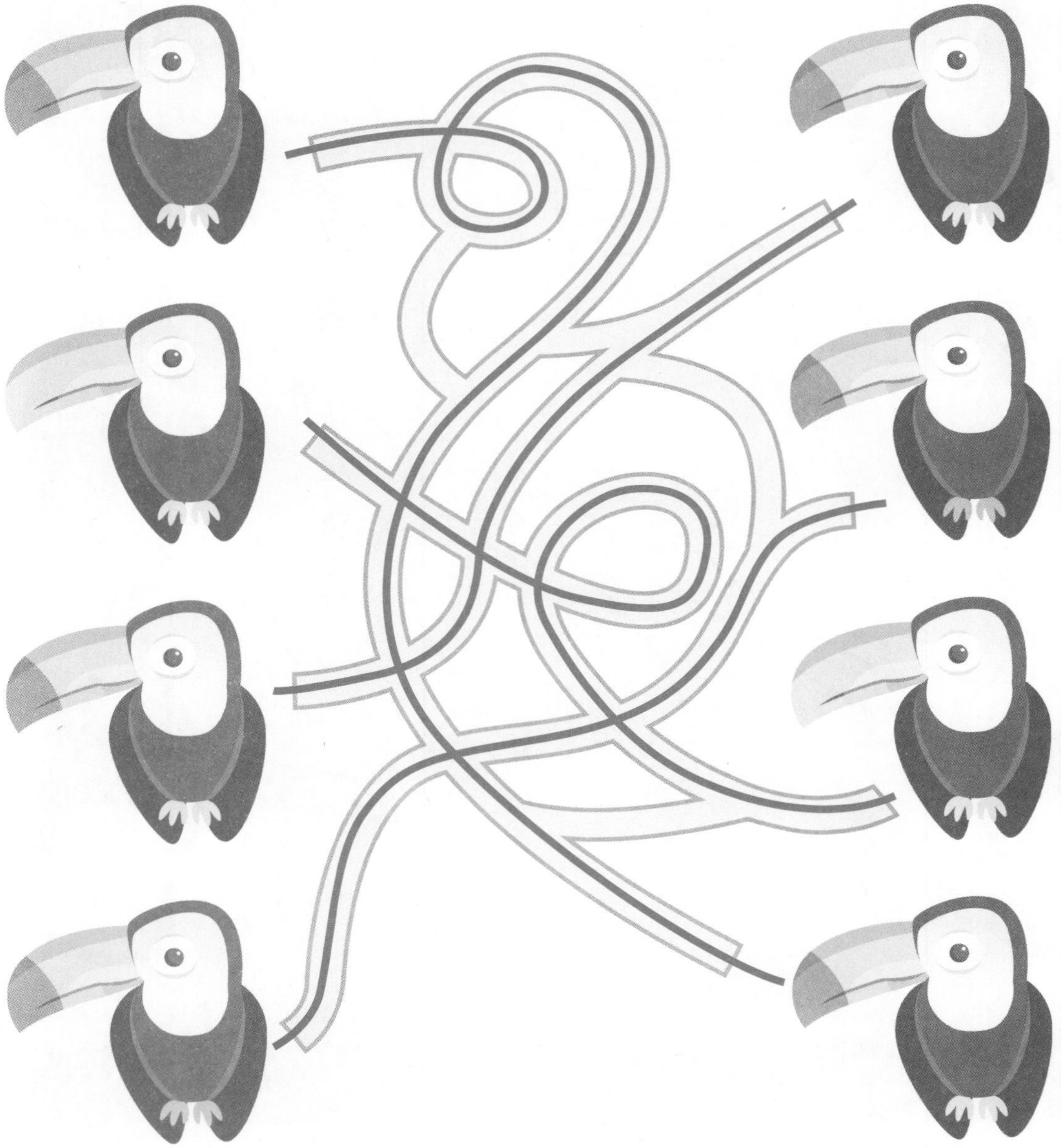

LET'S FIND WORDS!

Look at the puzzle and see if you can find each word listed. They all start with the letter **M**! Look for the words across and up and down.

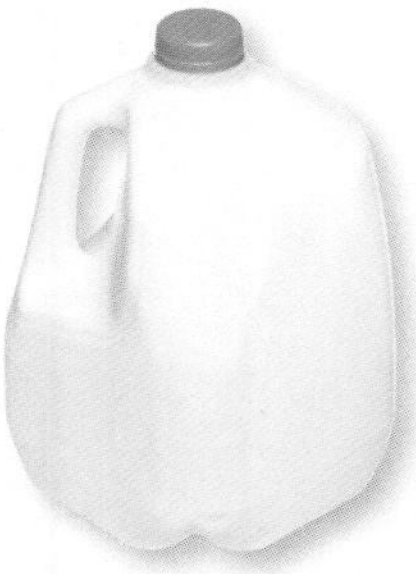

MILK

MONKEY

MARKER

MAT

WELCOME

MOUSE

MARBLES

E	A	T	M	C	X	W
F	A	P	O	I	M	I
M	A	R	B	L	E	S
M	O	N	K	E	Y	S
R	M	O	U	S	E	M
M	A	R	K	E	R	A
M	I	L	K	E	F	T

ANSWERS

LET'S FIND WORDS!

Look at the puzzle and see if you can find each word listed. They all start with the letter **M**! Look for the words across and up and down.

MILK

MONKEY

MARKER

WELCOME

MAT

MOUSE

MARBLES

E	A	T	M	C	X	W
F	A	P	O	I	M	I
M	A	R	B	L	E	S
M	O	N	K	E	Y	S
R	M	O	U	S	E	M
M	A	R	K	E	R	A
M	I	L	K	E	F	T

SPOT THE DIFFERENCE IN THE OCEAN

Circle five things that are different in these two pictures.

ANSWERS

SPOT THE DIFFERENCE IN THE OCEAN

Circle five things that are different in these two pictures.

SECRET CODE

Shh! Use this secret code to answer this riddle:

What animal is smarter than a talking parrot?

1=S 3=N 5=P 7=A 9=I

2=B 4=L 6=E 8=G

Answer:

___ ___ ___ ___ ___ ___ ___ ___ ___

7 1 5 6 4 4 9 3 8

___ ___ ___

2 6 6

ABC

ANSWERS

SECRET CODE

Shh! Use this secret code to answer this riddle:

What animal is smarter than a talking parrot?

1=S 3=N 5=P 7=A 9=I

2=B 4=L 6=E 8=G

Answer:

A		S	P	E	L	L	I	N	G
7		1	5	6	4	4	9	3	8

B	E	E
2	6	6

ABC

CAN YOU FIND?

Search, find, and circle these things at the birthday party!

2 blue balloons

1 seashell

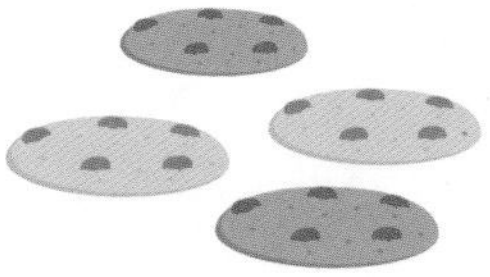

4 chocolate chip cookies

1 frog

3 envelopes

1 sock

H
A
P
P
Y
12
1
2
3
4
5
6
7
8
9
10
11

ANSWERS

CAN you FIND?

Search, find, and circle these things at the birthday party!

- 2 blue balloons
- 1 seashell
- 4 chocolate chip cookies
- 1 frog
- 3 envelopes
- 1 sock

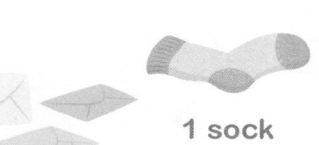

H
A
P
P
Y

PIZZA! TOPPINGS! YUMMY!

All three of those words have double letters.
Fill in the blanks to discover pizza
toppings that have double letters too!

CH__ __SE

MEATBA__ __S

GR__ __N PE__ __ERS

MUSHR__ __MS

BRO__ __OLI

LE__ __UCE

ANSWERS

PIZZA! TOPPINGS! YUMMY!

All three of those words have double letters.
Fill in the blanks to discover pizza
toppings that have double letters too!

CHEESE

MEATBALLS

GREEN PEPPERS

MUSHROOMS

BROCCOLI

LETTUCE

WHICH DOESN'T BELONG?

Which creature does **NOT** belong under the sea?

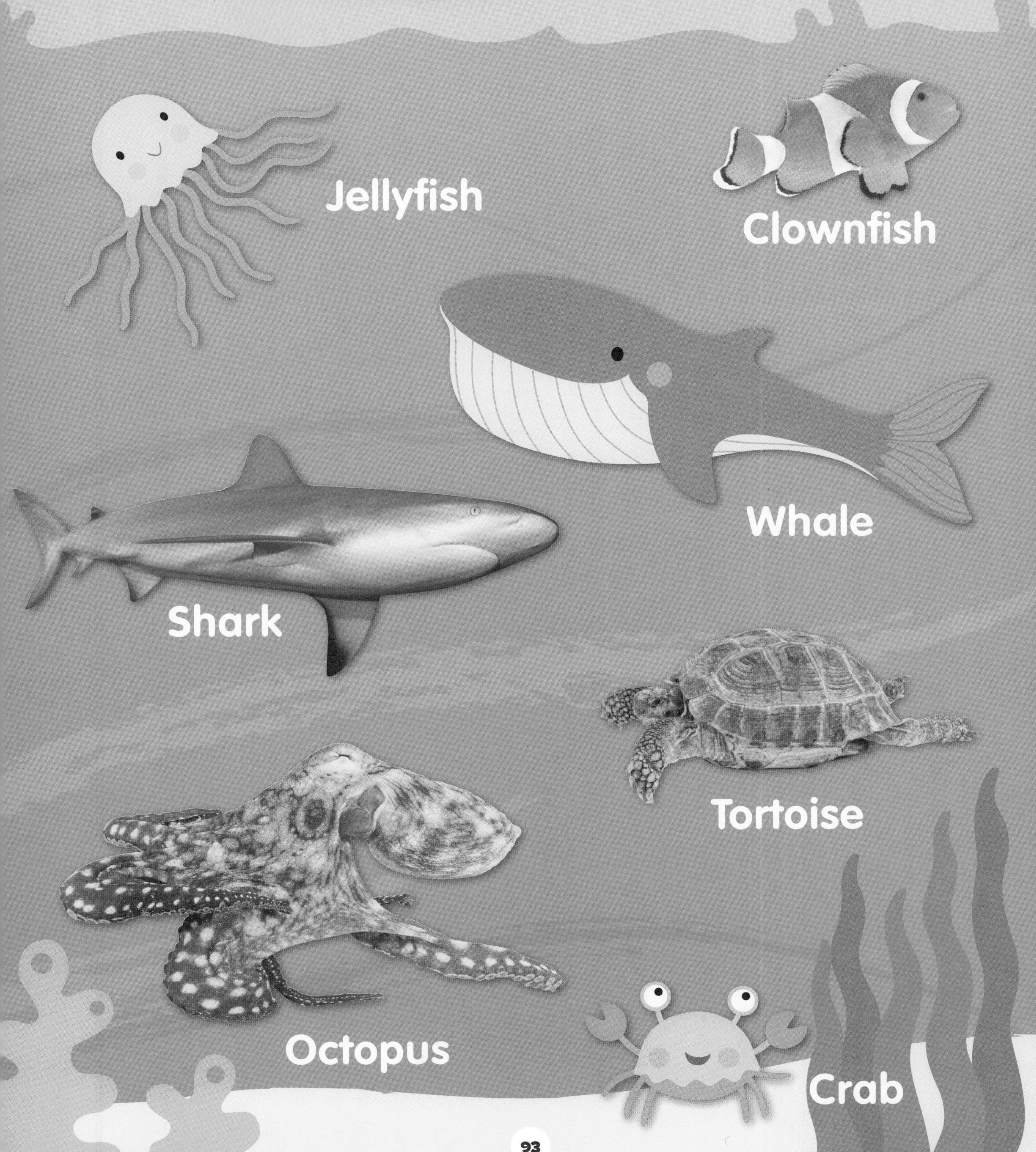
Jellyfish
Clownfish
Whale
Shark
Tortoise
Octopus
Crab

ANSWERS

WHICH DOESN'T BELONG?

Which creature does **NOT** belong under the sea?

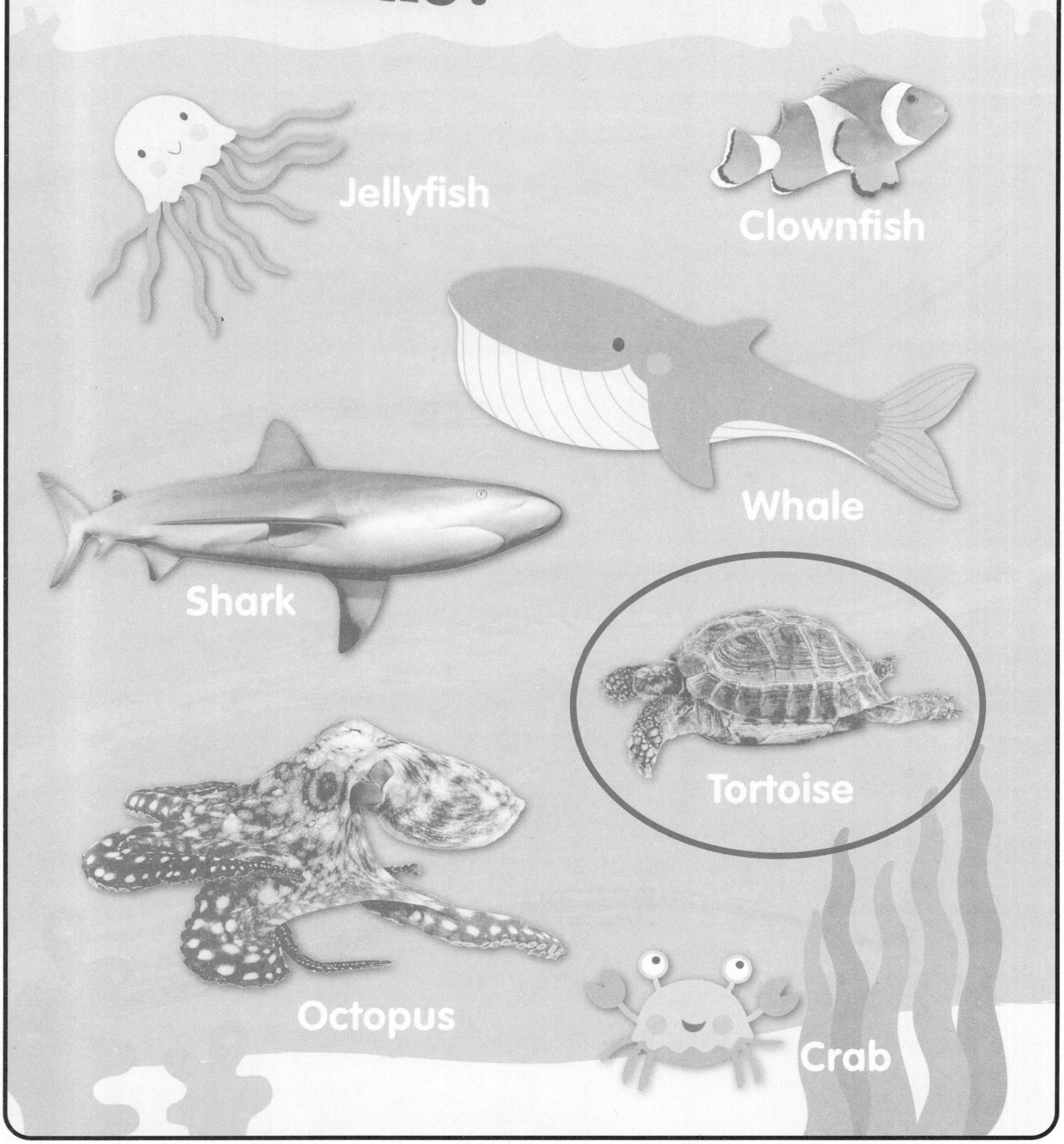
Jellyfish
Clownfish
Whale
Shark
Tortoise
Octopus
Crab

HAMMERHEAD SHARK

Look at these letters and see how many words you can make out of

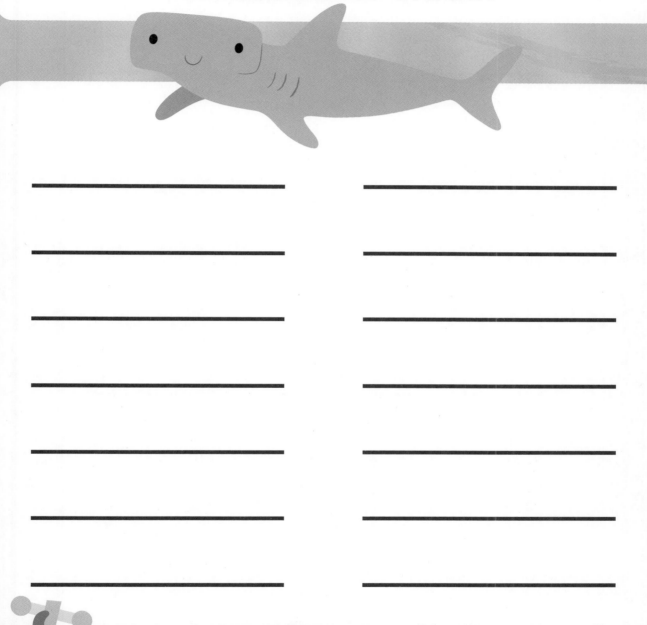

HAMMERHEAD SHARK

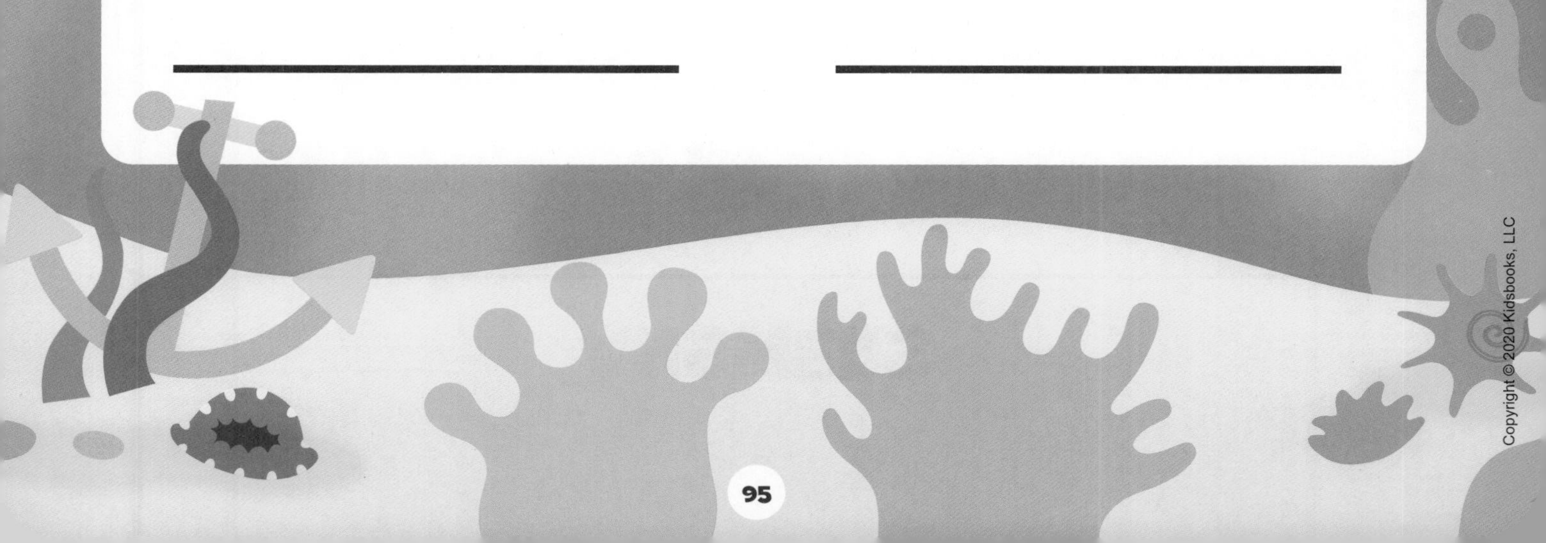

ANSWERS

HAMMERHEAD SHARK

Look at these letters and see how
many words you can make out of

HAMMERHEAD SHARK

Here are words you might have made:

MARK	HEAR
DEAR	READ
HAM	RED
DREAM	HAD
HEAD	MAKE
MASK	DARK
DESK	HARD

LET'S CIRCLE!

Circle five things that start with the letter **J**.

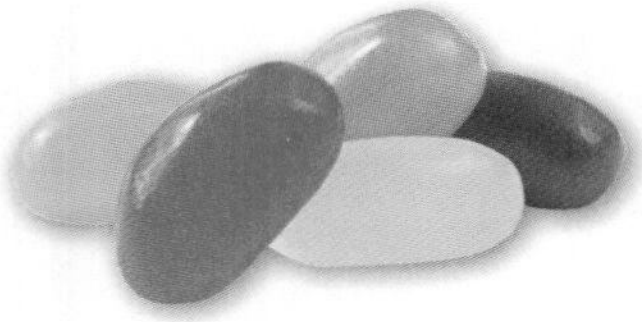

ANSWERS

LET'S CIRCLE!

Circle five things that start with the letter **J**.

WHAT'S WRONG?

Find five errors on this calendar page.

Octoober
Sunday
Tuesday
Tuesday
Wednesday
Thursday
Friday
Saturday
1 2 3 4 5 6 7
8 9 10 11 12 13 14
Halloween!
15 16 17 18 19 20 21
22 23 24 25 26 27 28
30 29 31

ANSWERS

WHAT'S WRONG?

Find five errors on this calendar page.

Octoober
Sunday Tuesday Tuesday Wednesday Thursday Friday Saturday
1 2 3 4 5 6 7
8 9 10 11 12 13 14
Halloween!
15 16 17 18 19 20 21
22 23 24 25 26 27 28
30 29 31

LET'S CELEBRATE!

Match the holiday to the right picture.

GROUNDHOG DAY

VALENTINE'S DAY

APRIL FOOL'S DAY

FOURTH OF JULY

HALLOWEEN

THANKSGIVING

TRUE LOVE

ANSWERS

LET'S CELEBRATE!

Match the holiday to the right picture.

GROUNDHOG DAY

VALENTINE'S DAY

APRIL FOOL'S DAY

FOURTH OF JULY

HALLOWEEN

THANKSGIVING

TRUE LOVE

YOU'RE INVITED!

This birthday party invitation has a big mistake!
Use the alphabet code to figure out **WHERE** to go.

A=Z
B=Y
C=X
D=W
E=V
F=U
G=T
H=S
I=R
J=Q
K=P
L=O
M=N
N=M
O=L
P=K
Q=J
R=I
S=H
T=G
U=F
V=E
W=D
X=C
Y=B
Z=A

WHO: Your Friend!

WHY: To Celebrate a Birthday!

WHERE: YRT YLY'H YLDORMT

WHEN: Any Time You Get There!

Answer:

___ ___ ___
Y R T
,
___ ___ ___ ___
Y L Y H

___ ___ ___ ___ ___ ___ ___
Y L D O R M T

ANSWERS

YOU'RE INVITED!

This birthday party invitation has a big mistake!
Use the alphabet code to figure out **WHERE** to go.

A=Z
B=Y
C=X
D=W
E=V
F=U
G=T
H=S
I=R
J=Q
K=P
L=O
M=N
N=M
O=L
P=K
Q=J
R=I
S=H
T=G
U=F
V=E
W=D
X=C
Y=B
Z=A

WHO: Your Friend!

WHY: To Celebrate a Birthday!

WHERE: YRT YLY'H YLDORMT

WHEN: Any Time You Get There!

Answer:

B	I	G
Y	R	T

B	O	B	'S
Y	L	Y	H

B	O	W	L	I	N	G
Y	L	D	O	R	M	T

PARTY HAT TWINS

Draw a line to connect each party hat on the left to its exact twin on the right!

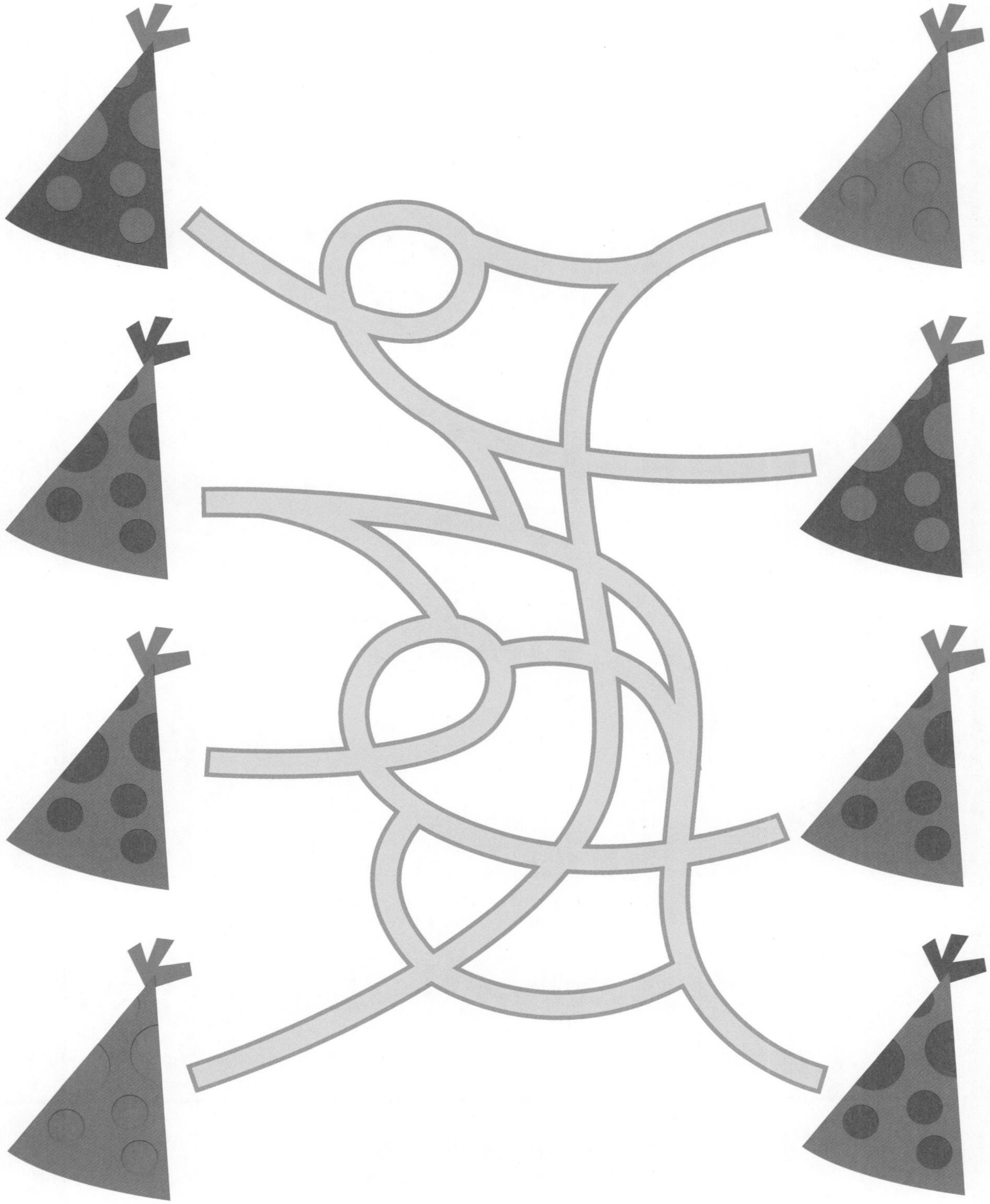

ANSWERS

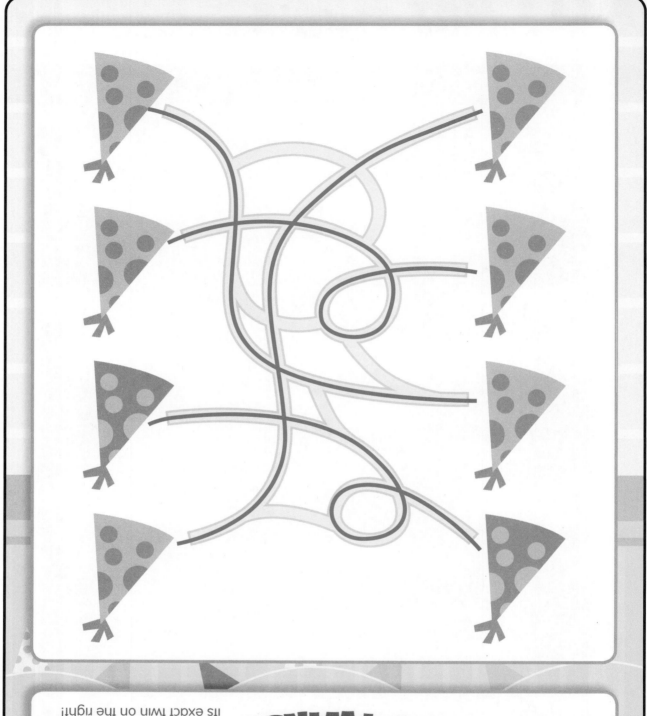

PARTY HAT TWINS

Draw a line to connect each party hat on the left to its exact twin on the right!

LET'S FIND WORDS!

Look at the puzzle and see if you can find each word listed. They all start with the letter **S**! Look for the words across and up and down.

STAR

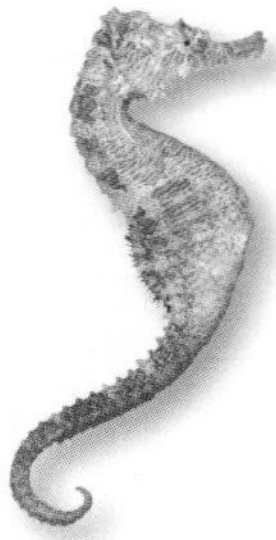

SEAHORSE

SNAKE

SCARF

SNOWMAN

STOP

STOP

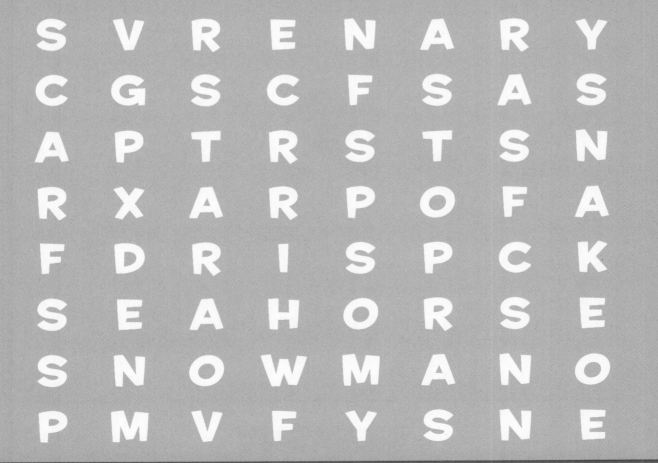

S	V	R	E	N	A	R	Y
C	G	S	C	F	S	A	S
A	P	T	R	S	T	S	N
R	X	A	R	P	O	F	A
F	D	R	I	S	P	C	K
S	E	A	H	O	R	S	E
S	N	O	W	M	A	N	O
P	M	V	F	Y	S	N	E

ANSWERS

LET'S FIND WORDS!

Look at the puzzle and see if you can find each word listed. They all start with the letter **S**! Look for the words across and up and down.

STAR

SEAHORSE

SNAKE

SCARF

SNOWMAN

STOP

STOP

S	V	R	E	N	A	R	Y
C	G	S	C	F	S	A	S
A	P	T	R	S	T	S	N
R	X	A	R	P	O	F	A
F	D	R	I	S	P	C	K
S	E	A	H	O	R	S	E
S	N	O	W	M	A	N	O
P	M	V	F	Y	S	N	E

SPOT THE DIFFERENCE IN MONSTER TOWN

Circle five things that are different in these two pictures.

Bigfoot Toys
Monster Dance Studio
TAXI
TAXI

Toys
Monster Dance Studio
TAXI

ANSWERS

SPOT THE DIFFERENCE IN MONSTER TOWN

Circle five things that are different in these two pictures.

Bigfoot Toys
Monster Dance Studio
TAXI
TAXI

Toys
Monster Dance Studio
TAXI

LET'S GO TO THE ZOO!

The word zoo has double letters.
Fill in the blank spaces to discover zoo
animals that have double letters, too.

ZOO

A__ __IGATOR

HI__ __O

M__ __SE

CH__ __TAH

BAB__ __N

GORI__ __A

GIRA__ __E

KANGAR__ __

ANSWERS

LET'S GO TO THE ZOO!

The word zoo has double letters.
Fill in the blank spaces to discover zoo
animals that have double letters, too.

A L L I G A T O R

ZOO

H I P P O

M O O S E

C H E E T A H

B A B O O N

G O R I L L A

G I R A F F E

K A N G A R O O

FIX 'N' MATCH

Unscramble the words on the left.
Then match each word to its picture on the right.
They are all things you see at the beach!

EACHB ABLL ________________ ○

SEALLEHS ________________ ○

AWSVE ________________ ○

BOOIEG RDOAB ________________ ○

WELTO ________________ ○

ANDS ________________ ○

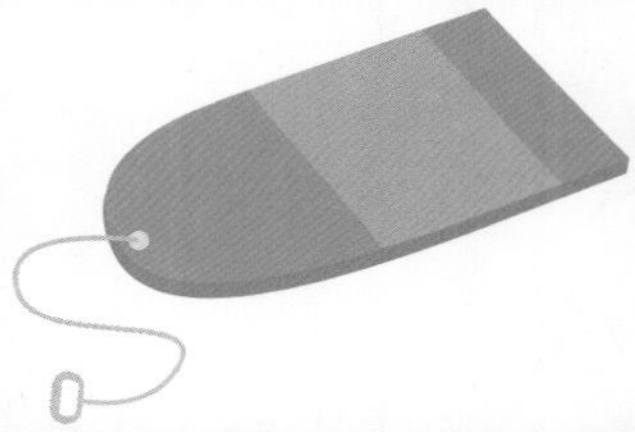

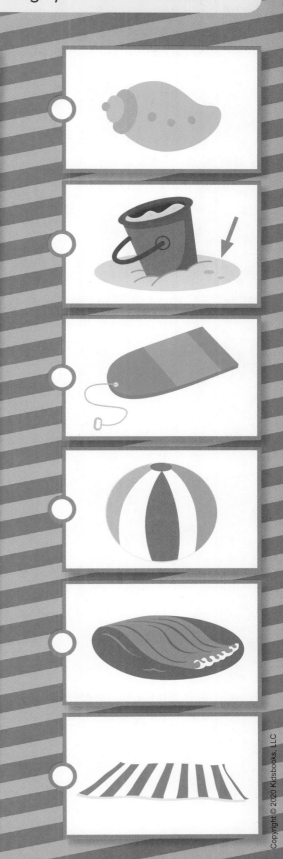

ANSWERS

FIX 'N' MATCH

Unscramble the words on the left.
Then match each word to its picture on the right.
They are all things you see at the beach!

EACHB ABLL ___BEACH BALL___

SEALLEHS ___SEASHELL___

AWSVE ___WAVES___

BOOIEG RDOAB ___BOOGIE BOARD___

WELTO ___TOWEL___

ANDS ___SAND___

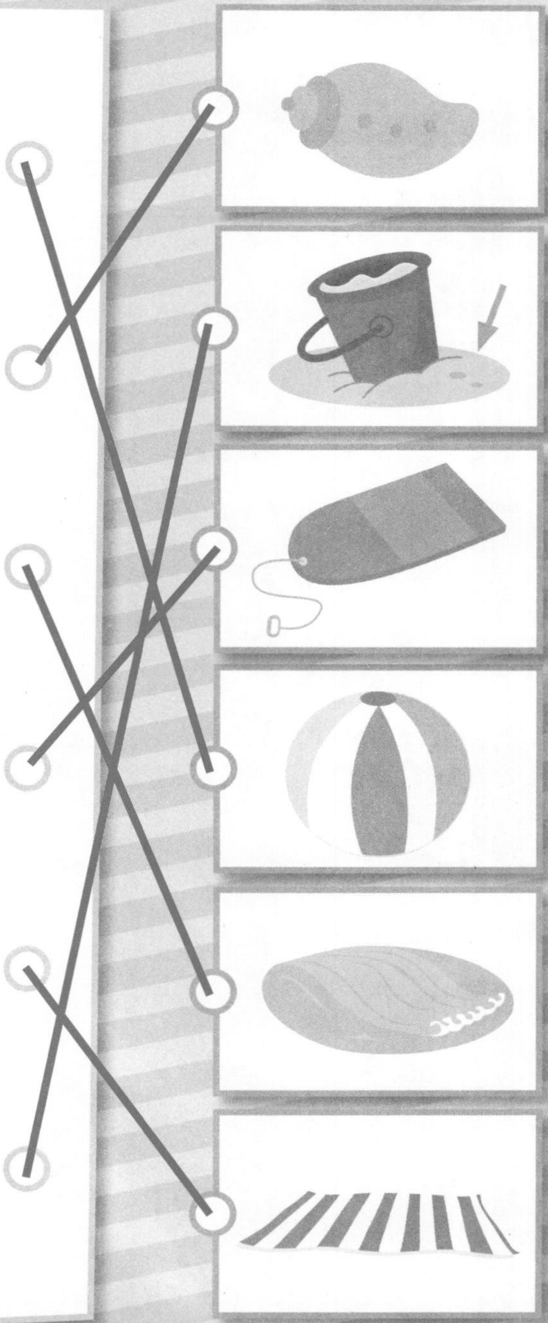

LOOK-ALIKES

Which two surfing monsters are exactly the same?

ANSWERS

LOOK-ALIKES

Which two surfing monsters are exactly the same?

SUMMER VACATION

What a great time of year!
See how many words you can make out of

SUMMER VACATION

ANSWERS

SUMMER VACATION

What a great time of year!
See how many words you can make out of

SUMMER VACATION

Here are words you might have made:

TRACE	VOTE
ACTOR	OUT
NEAT	NEAR
TRAIN	TIRES
SUIT	SOUR
STAIR	REST
NURSE	NEST

RIDDLE TIME!

Write the first letter of each object to answer this riddle:

What is as big as an elephant but doesn't weigh anything?

___ ___ ___

 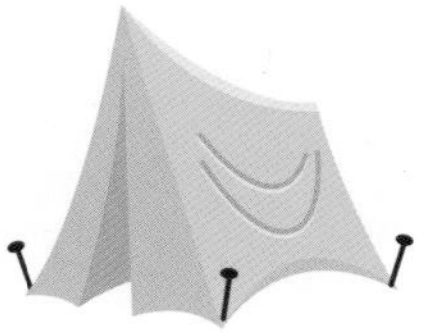 

___ ___ ___ ___ ___ ___

   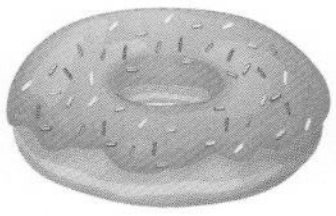  

Answer:

____

ANSWERS

RIDDLE TIME!

Write the first letter of each object to answer this riddle:

What is as big as an elephant but doesn't weigh anything?

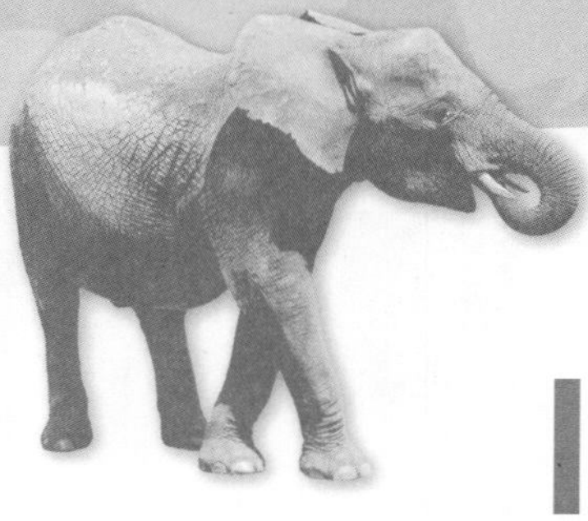

I T S

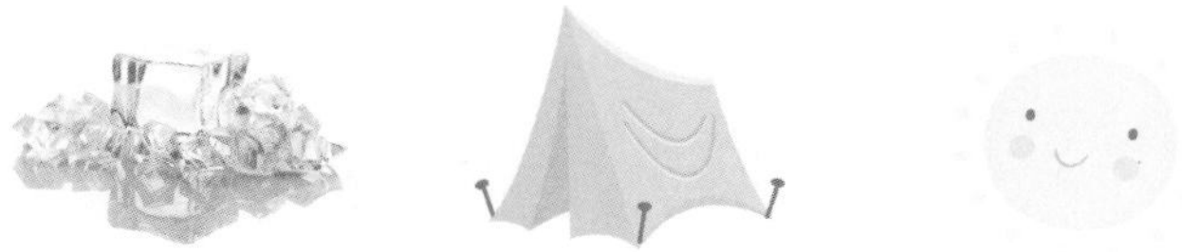

S H A D O W

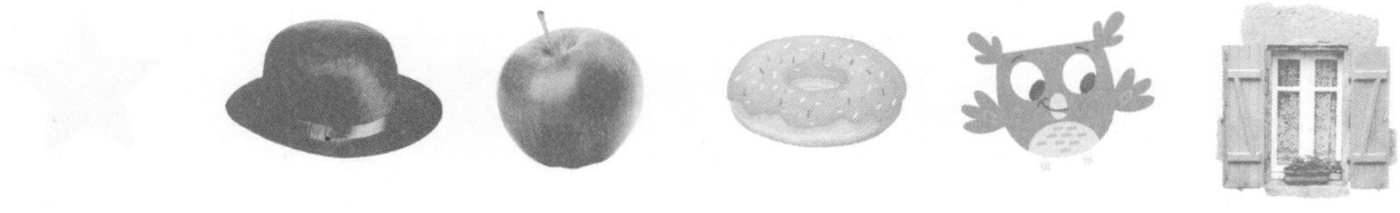

Answer:

ITS SHADOW

NAME THE OPPOSITE

Use the clues to complete this crossword puzzle.
Each answer is the opposite of the clue.

ACROSS

3. sad
4. slow

DOWN

1. down
2. big
3. cold

1.
2.
3.
4.

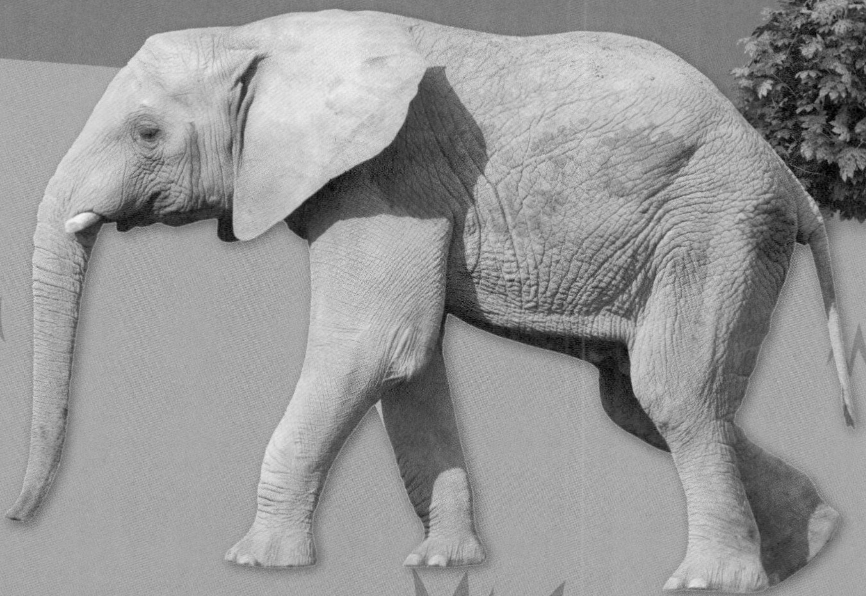

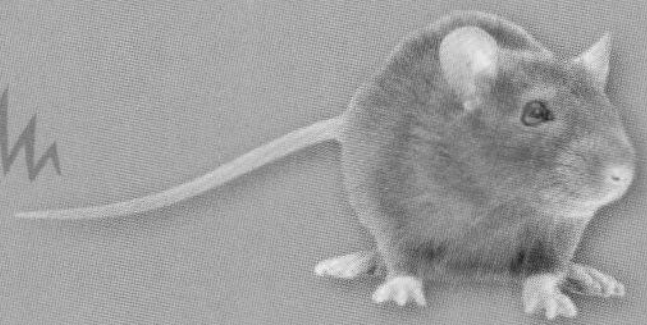

ANSWERS

NAME THE OPPOSITE

Use the clues to complete this crossword puzzle.
Each answer is the opposite of the clue.

ACROSS

3. sad 4. slow

DOWN

1. down 2. big 3. cold

1. U
2. S M A L L
3. H A P P Y
3. H O T
4. F A S T

DOT TO DOT

What is this shopper buying at the grocery store?
Connect the dots from 1 to 20 and find out!

MILK
1
2
3
4
5
6
7
8
9
10
11
12
13
14
15
16
17
18
19
20

ANSWERS

DOT TO DOT

What is this shopper buying at the grocery store?
Connect the dots from 1 to 20 and find out!

MILK
1
2
3
4
5
6
7
8
9
10
11
12
13
14
15
16
17
18
19
20

IT'S MAGIC!

Try this magic trick:
Turn a BOAT into a COIN.

You don't need a wand.
Just change one letter at a time to get different words.

BOAT 

 _OAT

_OA_ 

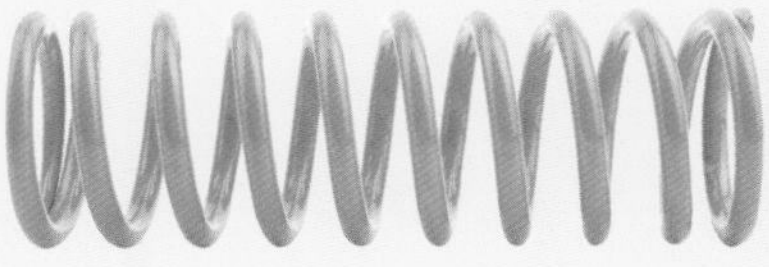 CO_ _

COI_ 

ANSWERS

IT'S MAGIC!

Try this magic trick:
Turn a BOAT into a COIN.

You don't need a wand.
Just change one letter at a time to get different words.

BOAT 

 **C**OAT

COA**L** 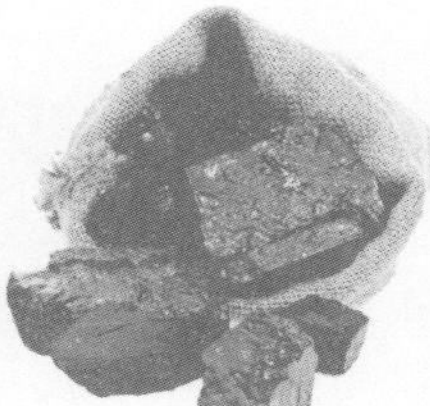

 CO**I** **L**

COI**N**

SPOT THE DIFFERENCE AT THE CAMPSITE

Circle five things that are different in these two pictures.

ANSWERS

SPOT THE DIFFERENCE AT THE CAMPSITE

Circle five things that are different in these two pictures.

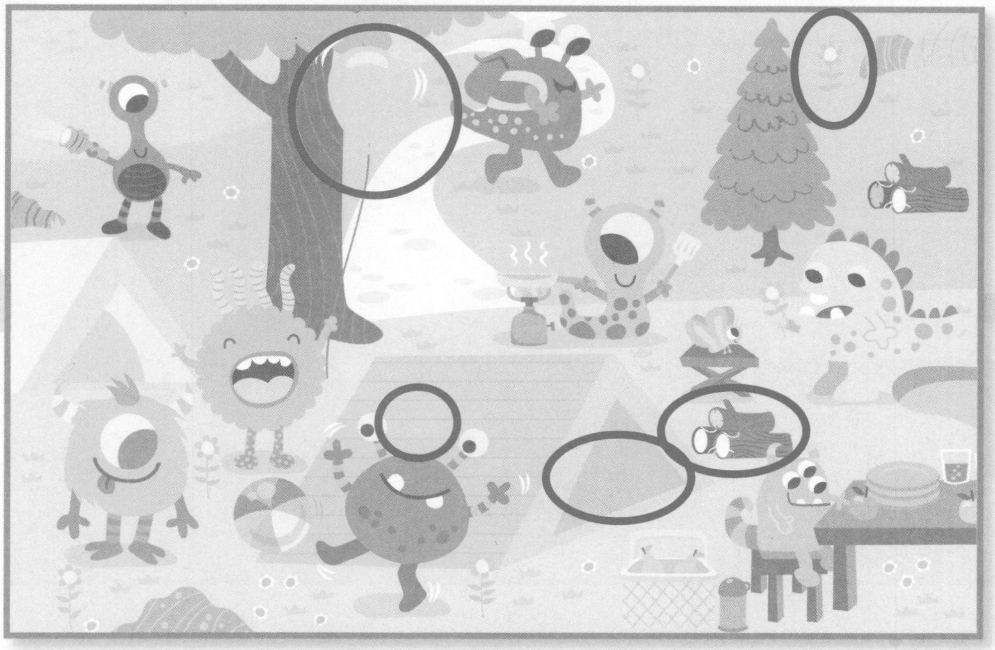

LOOK-ALIKES

Which two hot air balloons are exactly the same?

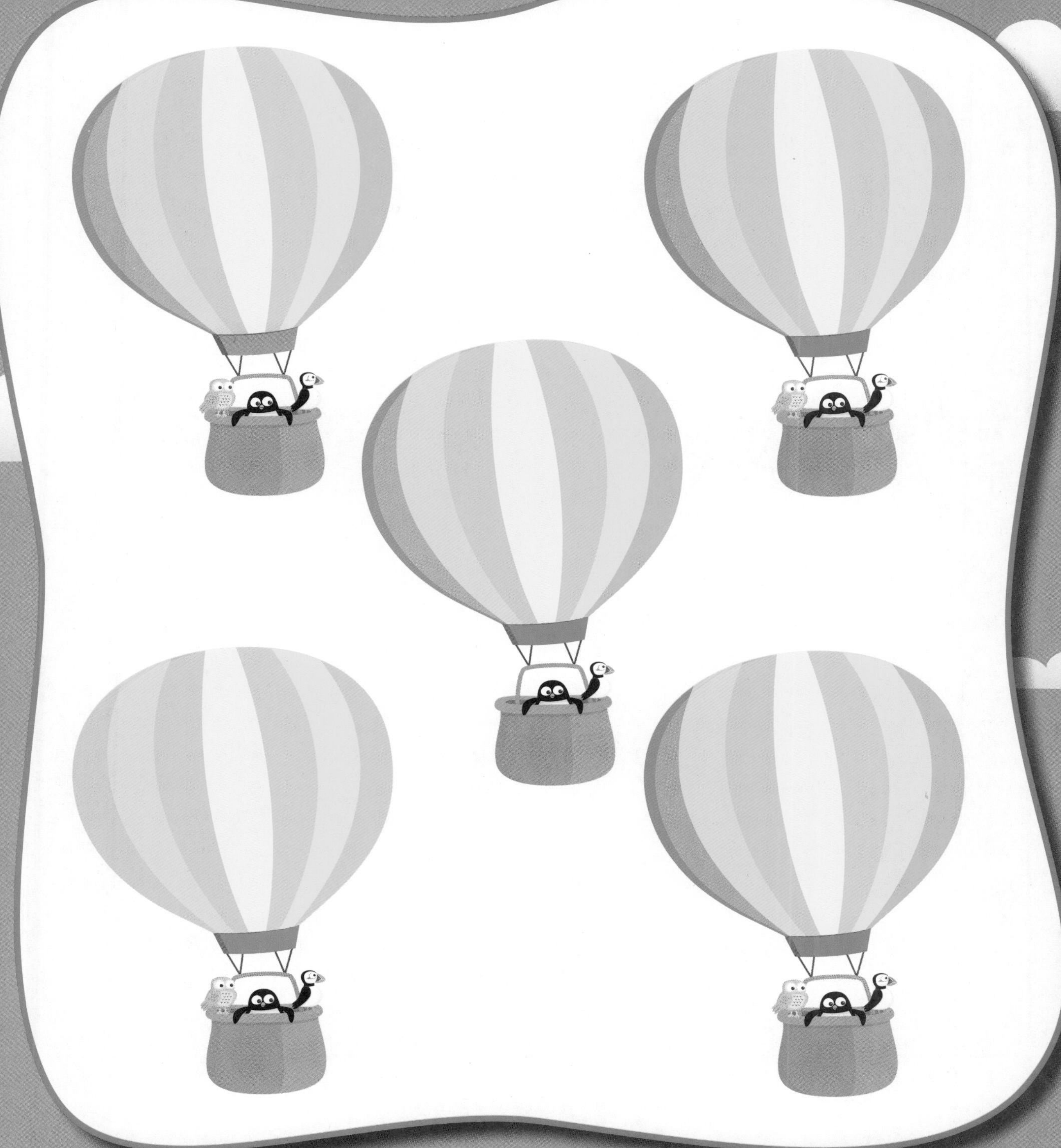

ANSWERS

LOOK-ALIKES

Which two hot air balloons are exactly the same?

REBUS FUN

Solve the rebus puzzle to answer this question:

Who invented the telephone?

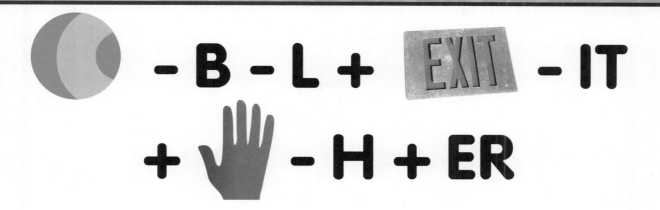

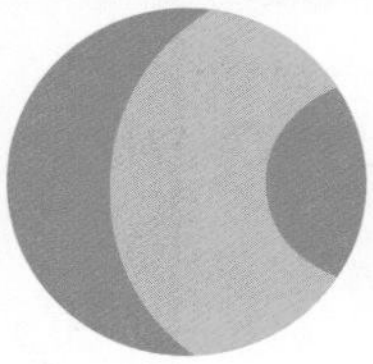 - B - L + 
EXIT
 - IT

+  - H + ER

__ __ __ __ __ __ __ __ __

 - PES + 

__ __ __ __ __ __

 - DOOR __ __ __ __

Answer:

__________ __________ __________

ANSWERS

REBUS FUN

Solve the rebus puzzle to answer this question:

Who invented the telephone?

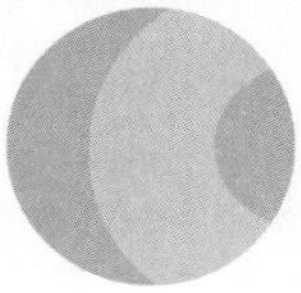 - B - L + 
EXIT
 - IT

+ 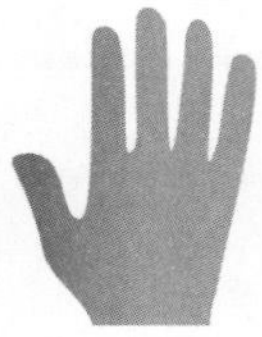 - H + ER

A L E X A N D E R

 - PES + 

G R A H A M

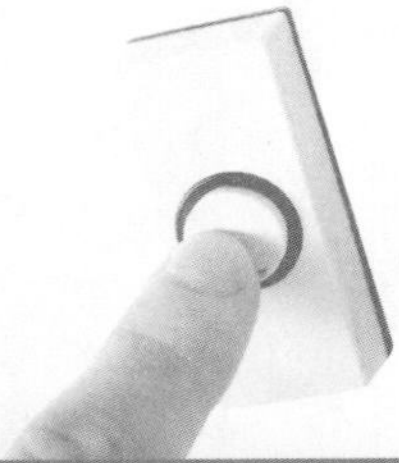 - DOOR B E L L

Answer:

ALEXANDER GRAHAM BELL

SCHOOL SUPPLIES

It's the first day of school!
See how many words you can make out of

SCHOOL SUPPLIES

ANSWERS

SCHOOL SUPPLIES

It's the first day of school!
See how many words you can make out of

SCHOOL SUPPLIES

Here are words you might have made:

SHOP	CHIP
CHESS	CHILL
POLISH	HOP
HOOP	CLIP
HIPS	LIP
HOPE	HOUSE
POPSICLE	SPICE

MAZE CRAZE CENTIPEDE!

This centipede has 100 legs. Help it count by 100s and fill in the missing numbers along the way!

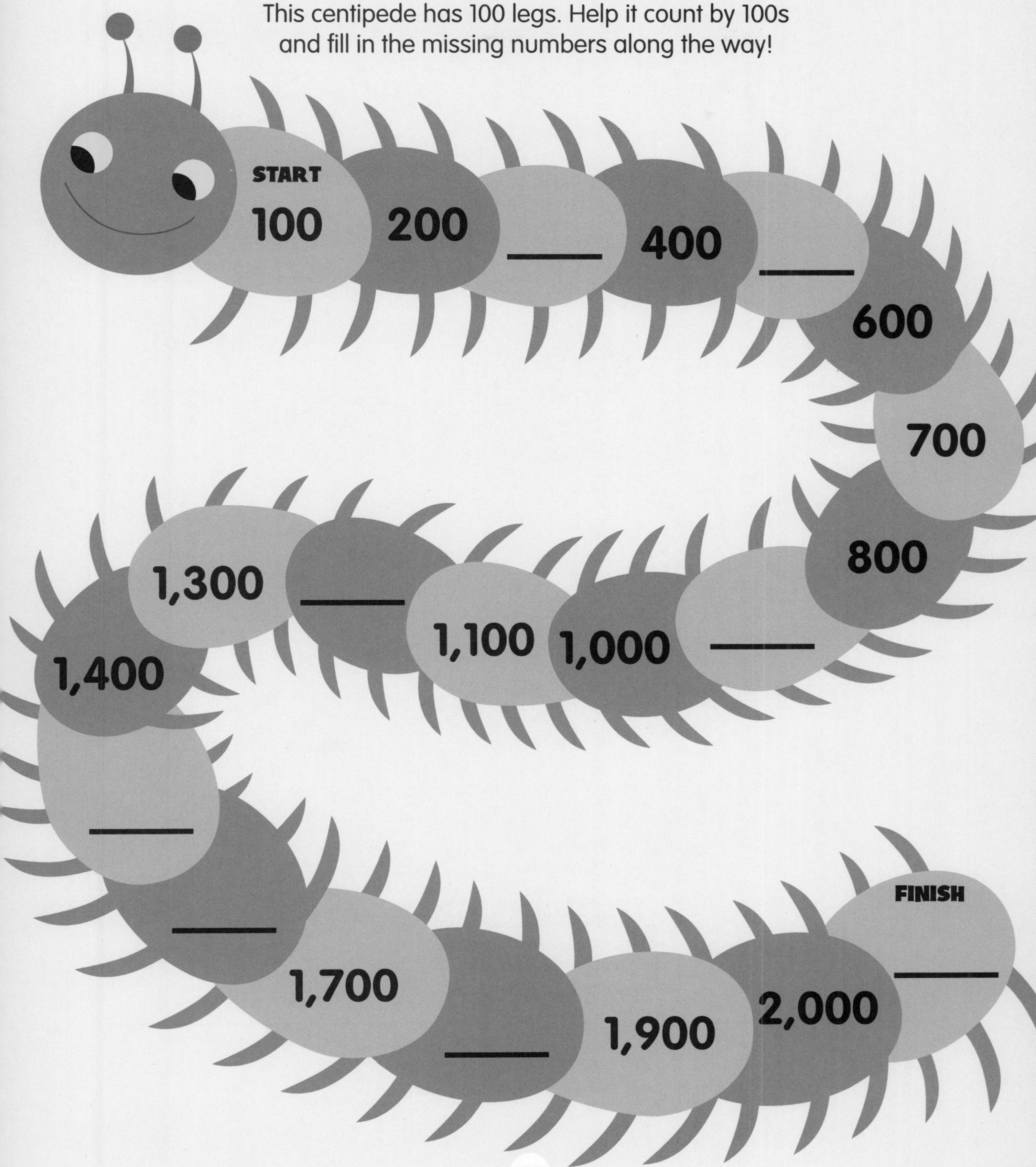
START
100
200
____
400
____
600
700
800
____
1,000
1,100
____
1,300
1,400
____
____
1,700
____
1,900
2,000
FINISH
____

ANSWERS

MAZE CRAZE CENTIPEDE!

This centipede has 100 legs. Help it count by 100s
and fill in the missing numbers along the way!

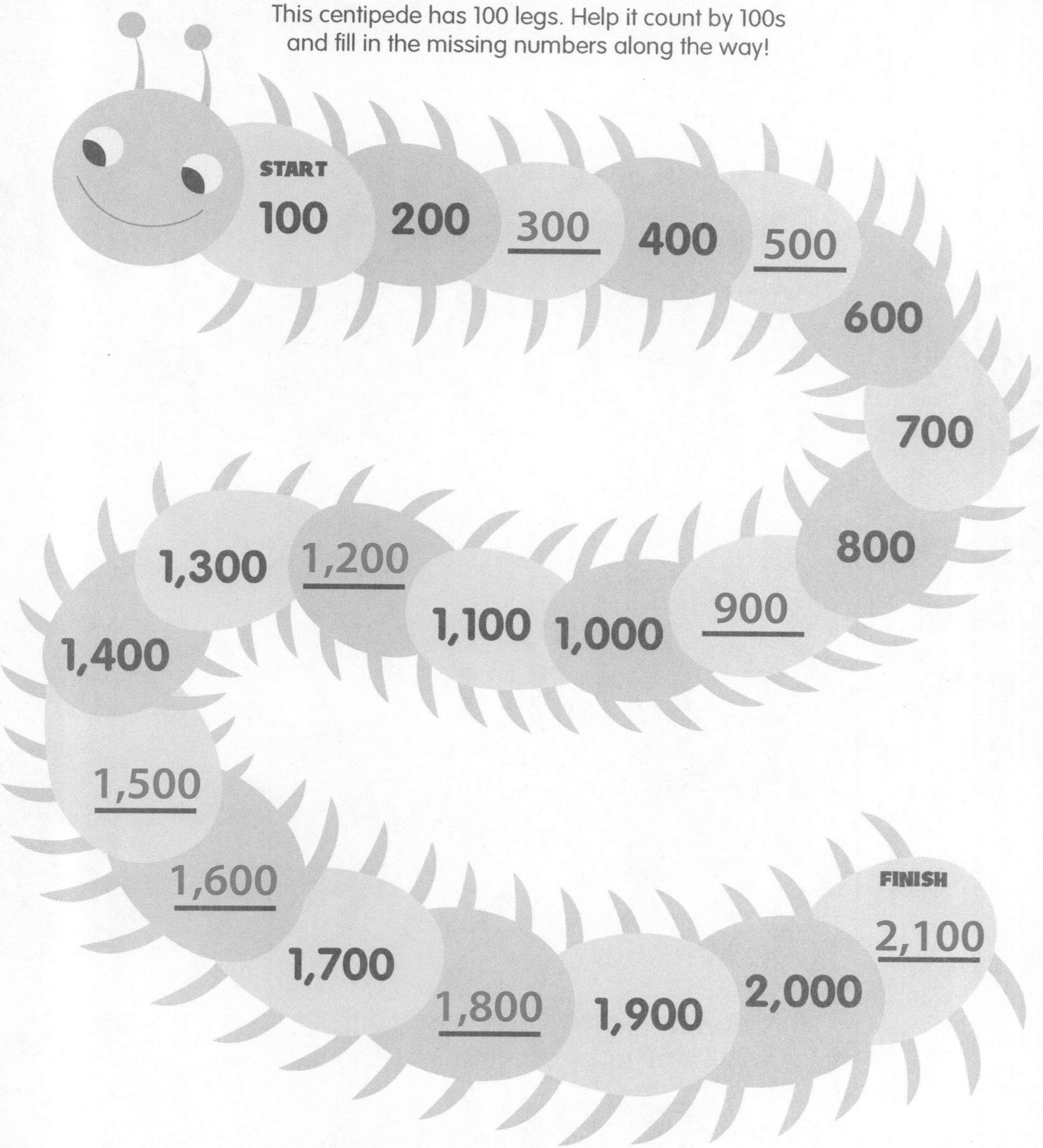

START
100
200
300
400
500
600
700
800
900
1,000
1,100
1,200
1,300
1,400
1,500
1,600
1,700
1,800
1,900
2,000
2,100
FINISH

FIX 'N' MATCH

Unscramble the words.
Then match each one to the right picture.
They are all musical instruments!

ARPH _____ ○

SMURD _____ ○

TMORENBO _____ ○

IANOP _____ ○

VINLIO _____ ○

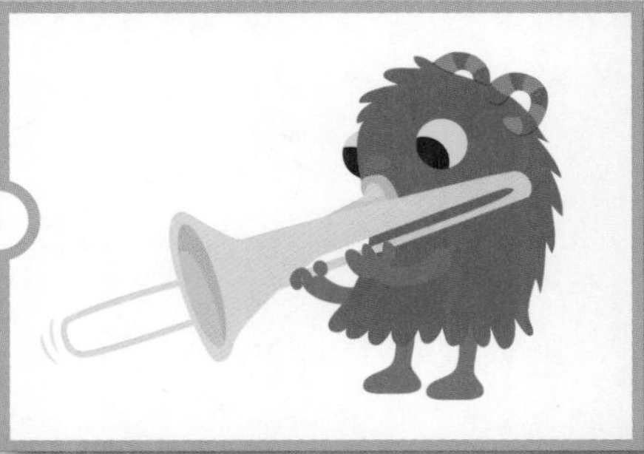

ANSWERS

FIX 'N' MATCH

Unscramble the words.
Then match each one to the right picture.
They are all musical instruments!

ARPH HARP

SMURD DRUMS

TMORENBO TROMBONE

IANOP PIANO

VINLIO VIOLIN

LET'S FIND WORDS!

Look at the puzzle and see if you can find each word listed. They are all pets! Look for the words across and up and down.

BIRD	CAT	GERBIL
BUNNY	DOG	HAMSTER

G	O	E	H	H	B	B
E	O	D	A	S	U	I
R	I	J	M	D	N	R
B	C	C	S	K	N	D
I	A	O	T	P	Y	P
L	T	O	E	D	O	G
L	I	B	R	A	M	V

ANSWERS

LET'S FIND WORDS!

Look at the puzzle and see if you can find each word listed. They are all pets! Look for the words across and up and down.

BIRD	CAT	GERBIL
BUNNY	DOG	HAMSTER

G	O	E	H	H	B	B
E	O	D	A	S	U	I
R	I	J	M	D	N	R
B	C	C	S	K	N	D
I	A	O	T	P	Y	P
L	T	O	E	D	O	G
L	I	B	R	A	M	V

SPOT THE DIFFERENCE AT THE AQUARIUM

Circle five things that are different in these two pictures.

ANSWERS

SPOT THE DIFFERENCE AT THE AQUARIUM

Circle five things that are different in these two pictures.

LET'S MAKE WORDS!

Write as many words as you can that start with the letter **N**.
Be creative! See if you can think of five words.

N ____________________

N ____________________

N ____________________

N ____________________

N ____________________

ANSWERS

LET'S MAKE WORDS!

Write as many words as you can that start with the letter **N**.
Be creative! See if you can think of five words.

Here are a few words:

NEST

NUMBER

NANNY

NUTS

NOWHERE

NAME THE NURSERY RHYME

Read the clues and fill in the blanks to complete the crossword puzzle.

ACROSS

1. Mary Had a Little ____________

2. Hey ____________, Diddle

DOWN

1. ____________ Bo Peep

3. This Little ____________

4. Hickory Dickory ____________

1
3
2
4

ANSWERS

NAME THE NURSERY RHYME

Read the clues and fill in the blanks to complete the crossword puzzle.

ACROSS

1. Mary Had a Little ______________

2. Hey ______________ , Diddle

DOWN

1. ______________ Bo Peep

3. This Little ______________

4. Hickory Dickory ______________

1 L A M B

I
T
T
L
E
3 P
2 D I D 4 D L E
G
G
Y
O
C
K

LET'S
CIRCLE!

Circle five things that start with the letter **Y**.

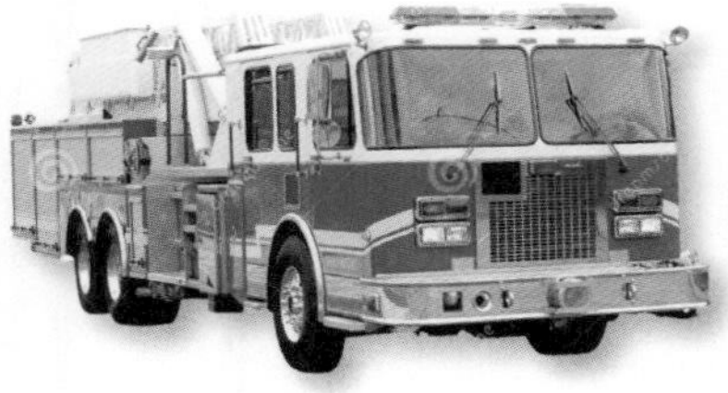

ANSWERS

LET'S CIRCLE!

Circle five things that start with the letter **Y**.

SECRET CODE

Shh! Use this secret code to answer this riddle:

What is the closest planet to the sun?

1=E	3=U	5=Y
2=R	4=M	6=C

Answer:

____ ____ ____ ____ ____ ____ ____

4 1 2 6 3 2 5

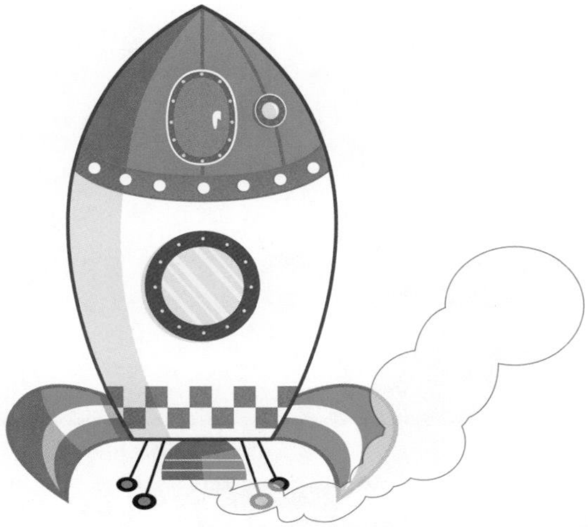

ANSWERS

SECRET CODE

Shh! Use this secret code to answer this riddle:

What is the closest planet to the sun?

1=E 3=U 5=Y
2=R 4=M 6=C

Answer:

M	E	R	C	U	R	Y
4	1	2	6	3	2	5

SOLAR SYSTEM

There are eight major planets in our solar system.
See how many words you can make out of

SOLAR SYSTEM

ANSWERS

SOLAR SYSTEM

There are eight major planets in our solar system.
See how many words you can make out of

SOLAR SYSTEM

Here are words you might have made:

MEAT	ARMY
ESSAY	ROYAL
YAM	LAYER
MAY	SMART
TEAR	TEARY
MY	STORM
TAME	TRAY

RIDDLE TIME!

Write the first letter of each object to answer this riddle:

What kind of music do planets like best?

___ ___ ___ -

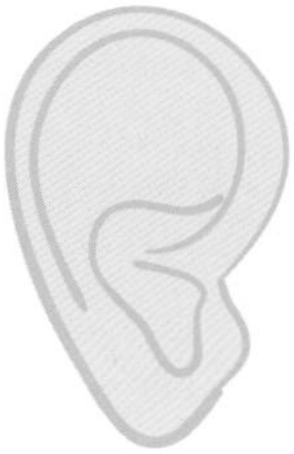

___ ___ ___ ___ ___

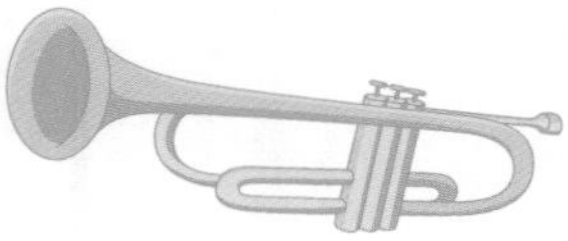

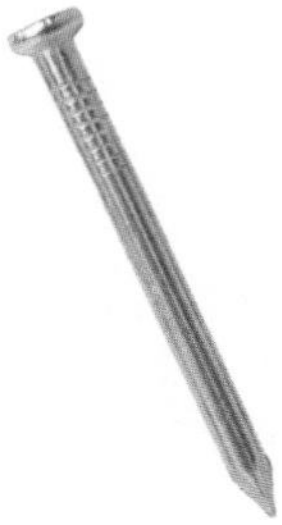

Answer:

________ - ________________

ANSWERS

RIDDLE TIME!

Write the first letter of each object to answer this riddle:

What kind of music do planets like best?

N E P -

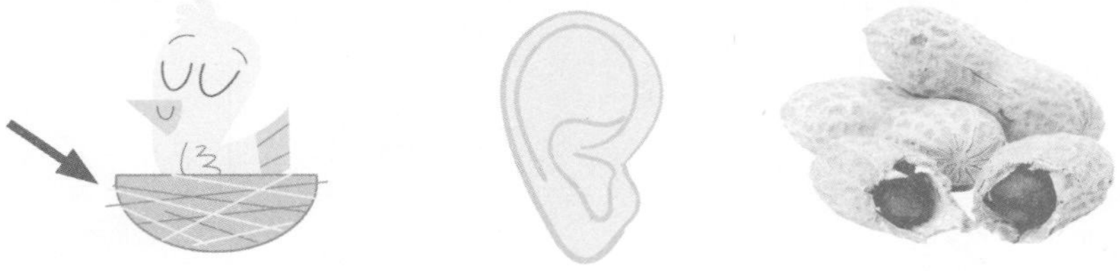

T U N E S

Answer:

NEP - TUNES

DOT TO DOT

Who is having fun with the whale?
Connect the dots from 1 to 35 and find out!

1 2 3 4 5 6 7 8 9 10 11 12 13 14 15 16 17 18 19 20 21 22 23 24 25 26 27 28 29 30 31 32 33 34 35

ANSWERS

DOT TO DOT

Who is having fun with the whale?
Connect the dots from 1 to 35 and find out!

33
3
32
2
4
6
5
7
28
27
26
24
22
21
14
16
15
18
17
12

WHICH IS DIFFERENT?

Find one grocery basket that is different from the rest.

ANSWERS

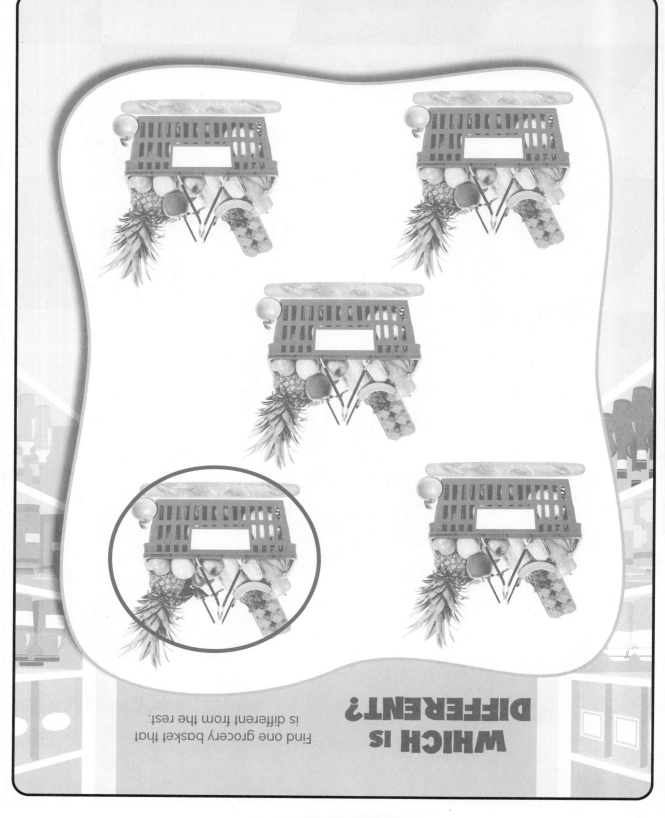

WHICH IS DIFFERENT?

Find one grocery basket that is different from the rest.

WORD TO WORD

Unscramble the words on the left, so they make one long word with the words on the right.

NUS

___ ___ ___ | ____________SHINE

ROOD

___ ___ ___ ___ | ____________BELL

FOTO

___ ___ ___ ___ | ____________BALL

RATS

___ ___ ___ ___ | ____________FISH

IDES

___ ___ ___ ___ | ____________WALK

MIAL

___ ___ ___ ___ | ____________BOX

ANSWERS

WORD TO WORD

Unscramble the words on the left, so they make one long word with the words on the right.

NUS	
S U N	SUN**SHINE**
ROOD	
D O O R	DOOR**BELL**
FOTO	
F O O T	FOOT**BALL**
RATS	
S T A R	STAR**FISH**
IDES	
S I D E	SIDE**WALK**
MIAL	
M A I L	MAIL**BOX**

LET'S FIND WORDS!

Look at the puzzle and see if you can find each word listed. They are things you see at the playground. Look for the words across and up and down.

BARS

SLIDE

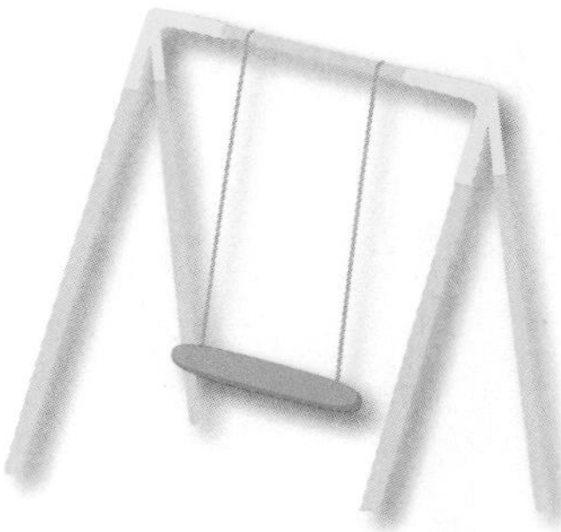

SWING

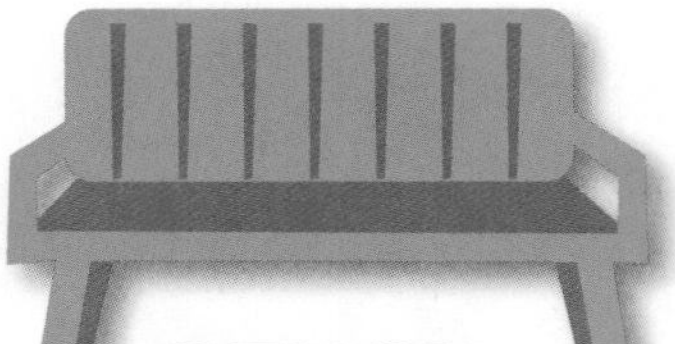

BENCH

SEESAW

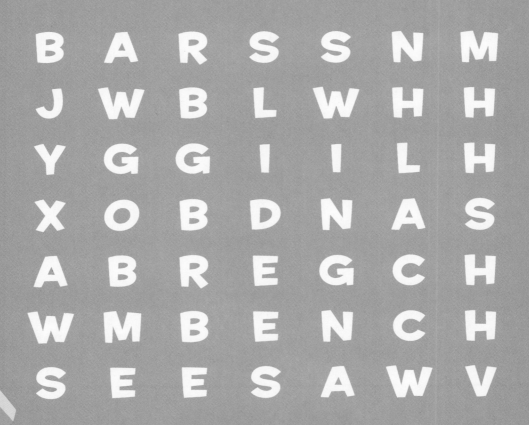

B	A	R	S	S	N	M
J	W	B	L	W	H	H
Y	G	G	I	I	L	H
X	O	B	D	N	A	S
A	B	R	E	G	C	H
W	M	B	E	N	C	H
S	E	E	S	A	W	V

ANSWERS

LET'S FIND WORDS!

Look at the puzzle and see if you can find each word listed. They are things you see at the playground. Look for the words across and up and down.

BARS

SLIDE

SWING

BENCH

SEESAW

B	A	R	S	S	N	M
J	W	B	L	W	H	H
Y	G	G	I	I	L	H
X	O	B	D	N	A	S
A	B	R	E	G	C	H
W	M	B	E	N	C	H
S	E	E	S	A	W	V

MAZE CRAZE MONEY!

Help this rich man bring his money to the bank.
The correct path is made up of only $100 bills.
You may not move diagonally.

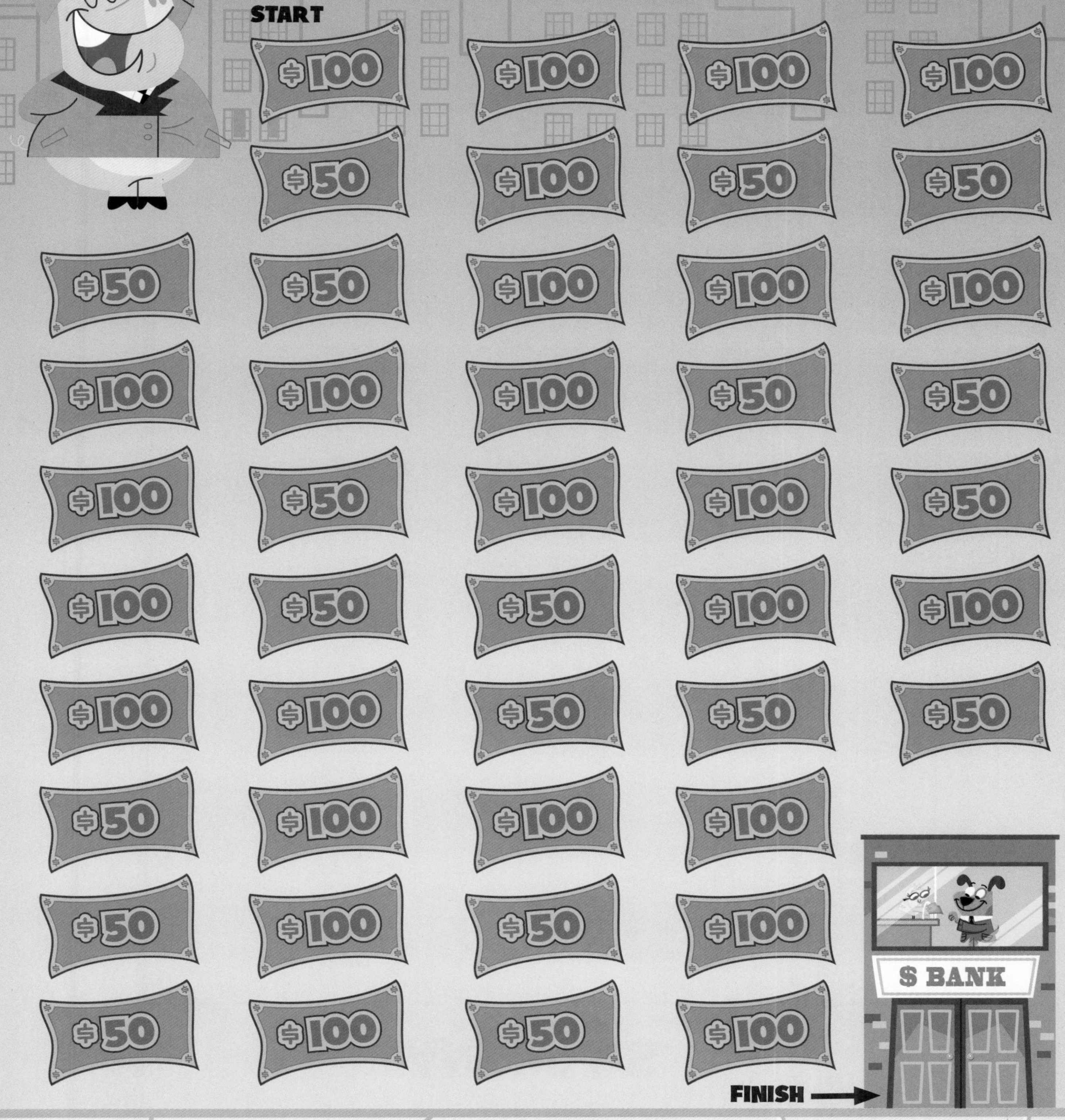
START
$100 $100 $100 $100
$50 $100 $50 $50
$50 $50 $100 $100 $100
$100 $100 $100 $50 $50
$100 $50 $100 $100 $50
$100 $50 $50 $100 $100
$100 $100 $50 $50 $50
$50 $100 $100 $100
$50 $100 $50 $100
$50 $100 $50 $100
$ BANK
FINISH

ANSWERS

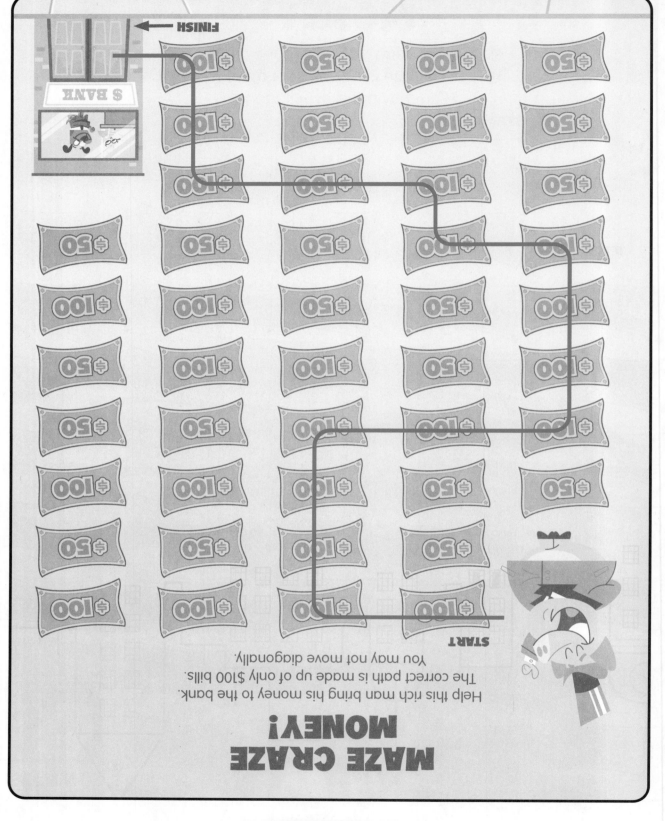

MAZE CRAZE MONEY!

Help this rich man bring his money to the bank.
The correct path is made up of only $100 bills.
You may not move diagonally.

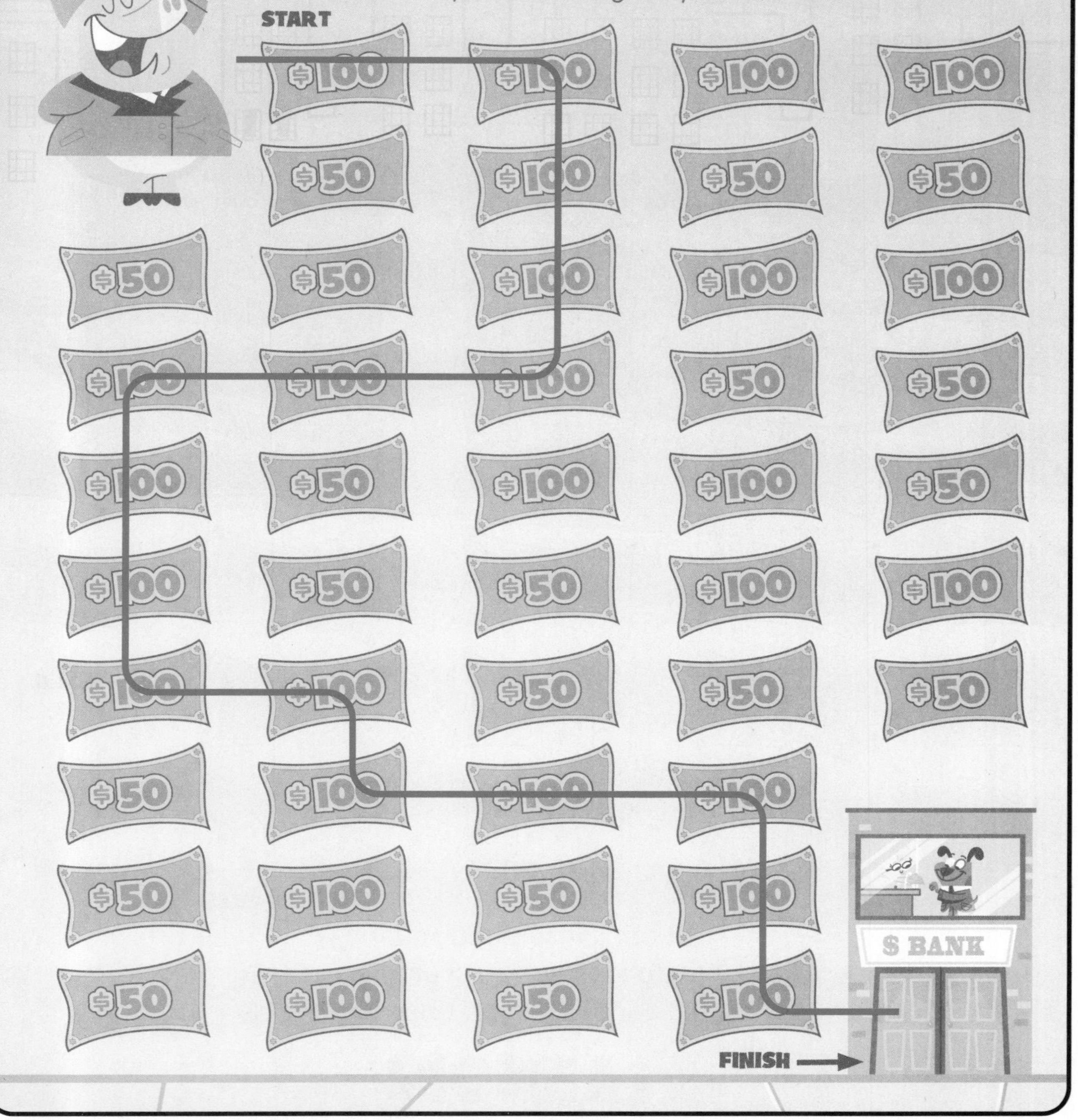
START
$ BANK
FINISH

SPOT THE DIFFERENCE ON THE FARM

Circle five things that are different in these two pictures.

ANSWERS

SPOT THE DIFFERENCE ON THE FARM

Circle five things that are different in these two pictures.

DOT TO DOT

Who came to welcome the brand new chicks?
Connect the dots from 1 to 40 and find out!

ANSWERS

DOT TO DOT

Who came to welcome the brand new chicks?
Connect the dots from 1 to 40 and find out!

PARROT TWINS

Draw a line to connect each parrot on the left to its exact twin on the right.

ANSWERS

PARROT TWINS

Draw a line to connect each parrot on the left to its exact twin on the right.

WORD TO WORD

Unscramble the words on the left, so they make one long word with the words on the right.

RIA ___ ___ ___	____________PLANE
TESKA ___ ___ ___ ___ ___	____________BOARD
WSNO ___ ___ ___ ___	____________MAN
EBD ___ ___ ___	____________ROOM
PCU ___ ___ ___	____________CAKE
SEAB ___ ___ ___ ___	____________BALL

ANSWERS

WORD TO WORD

Unscramble the words on the left, so they make one long word with the words on the right.

RIA: A I R	AIRPLANE
TESKA: S K A T E	SKATEBOARD
WSNO: S N O W	SNOWMAN
EBD: B E D	BEDROOM
PCU: C U P	CUPCAKE
SEAB: B A S E	BASEBALL

LET'S MAKE WORDS!

Write as many words as you can that start with the letter **I**.
Be creative! See if you can think of five words.

I ______________________________

I ______________________________

I ______________________________

I ______________________________

I ______________________________

ANSWERS

LET'S MAKE WORDS!

Write as many words as you can that start with the letter **I**.
Be creative! See if you can think of five words.

Here are a few words:

IGLOO

ICE CREAM

INSECT

IGUANA

INDOORS

CAN YOU FIND?

Search, find, and circle these things at the park!

2 butterflies

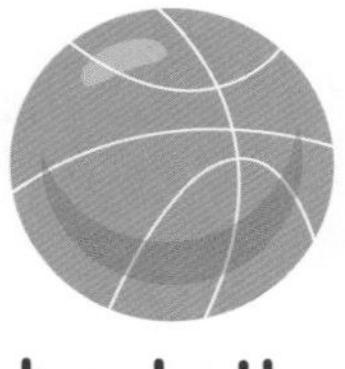

1 basketball

3 red flowers

2 ice-cream cones

4 birds

1 kite

ANSWERS

CAN YOU FIND?
Search, find, and circle these things at the park!
2 butterflies
1 basketball
3 red flowers
2 ice-cream cones
4 birds
1 kite

LET'S CIRCLE!

Circle five things that start with the letter **P**.

POP CORN
POP CORN

ANSWERS

LET'S CIRCLE!

Circle five things that start with the letter **P**.

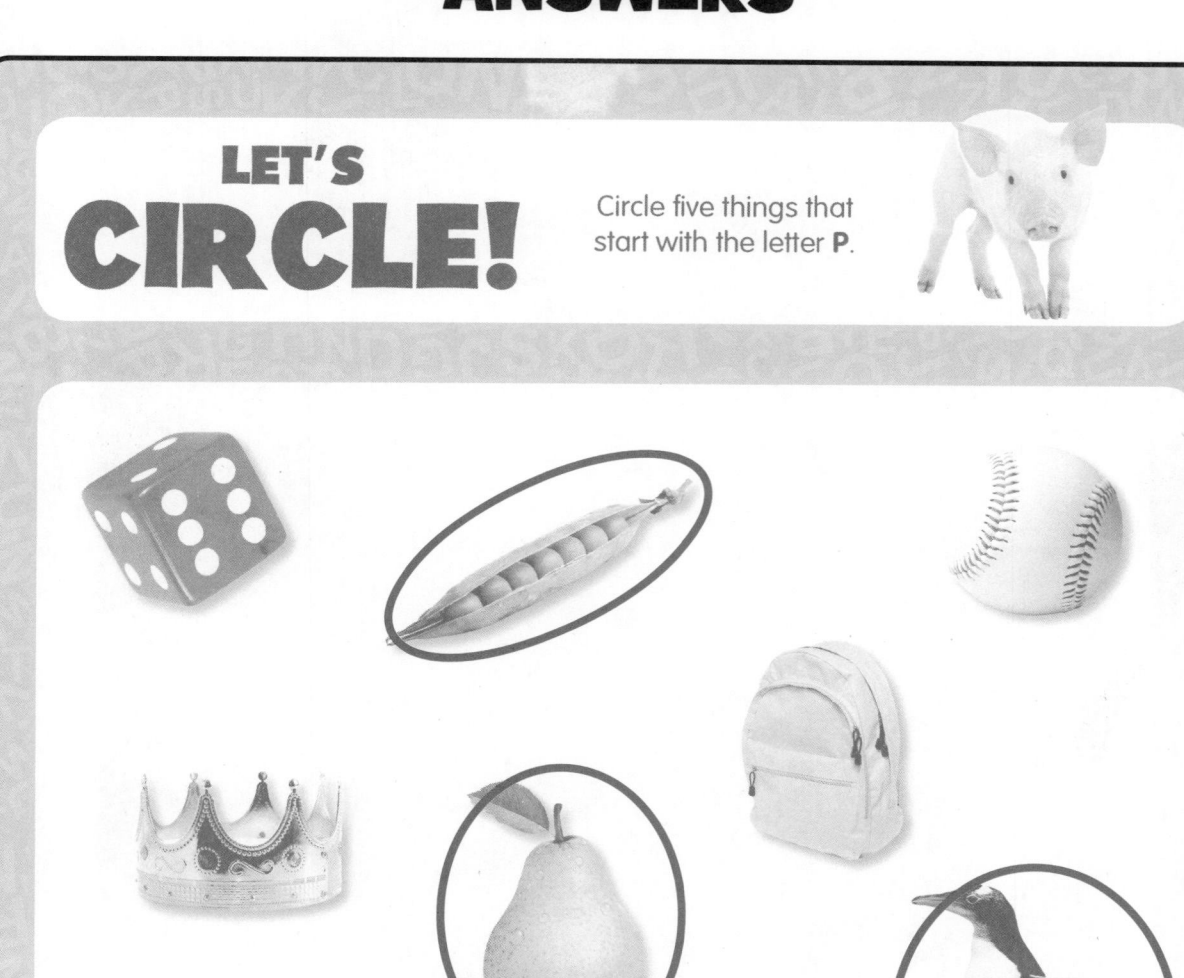

POP CORN
POP CORN

SECRET CODE

Shh! Use this secret code to answer this riddle:

What did the hat say to the hat rack?

1=G 3=I 5=A 7=E 9=D

2=N 4=H 6=L 8=O

Answer:

"YOU STAY HERE —

"__ __ __' __ __

3 6 6 1 8

__ __ __ __ __ __ __"

8 2 5 4 7 5 9

ANSWERS

SECRET CODE

Shh! Use this secret code to answer this riddle:

What did the hat say to the hat rack?

1=G 3=I 5=A 7=E 9=D

2=N 4=H 6=L 8=O

Answer:

"YOU STAY HERE —

"I	' L	L		G	O
3	6	6		1	8

O	N		A	H	E	A	D"
8	2		5	4	7	5	9

LET'S CIRCLE!

Circle five things that start with the letter **A**.

12
9
3
6

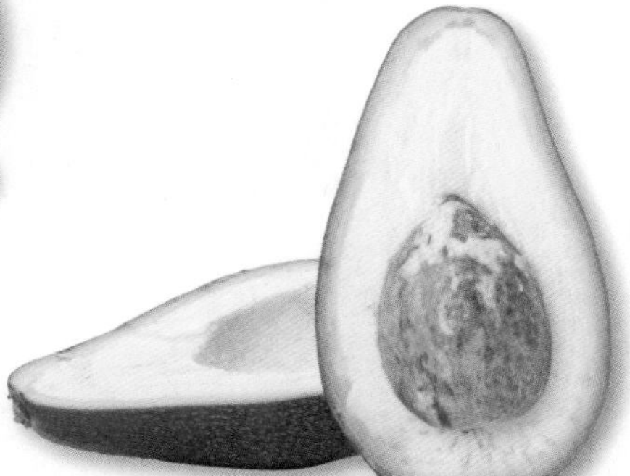

ANSWERS

LET'S CIRCLE!

Circle five things that start with the letter **A**.

12
9
3
6

MAZE CRAZE
IT'S ODD!

Meet Odd Todd. Help him find his way to Odd School.
The correct path is made up of only odd numbers.
But watch out! The numbers are not in order!
You may not move diagonally.

START

	3	7	9	8	6	10
14	4	2	15	1	12	14
1	7	3	2	13	5	9
15	4	5	11	7	8	11
13	9	6	12	10	2	4
14	3	11	7	13	**FINISH →**	

ANSWERS

MAZE CRAZE IT'S ODD!

Meet Odd Todd. Help him find his way to Odd School.
The correct path is made up of only odd numbers.
But watch out! The numbers are not in order!
You may not move diagonally.

START

	3	7	9	8	6	10
14	4	2	15	1	12	14
1	7	3	2	13	5	9
15	4	5	11	7	8	11
13	9	6	12	10	2	4
14	3	11	7	13		

FINISH →

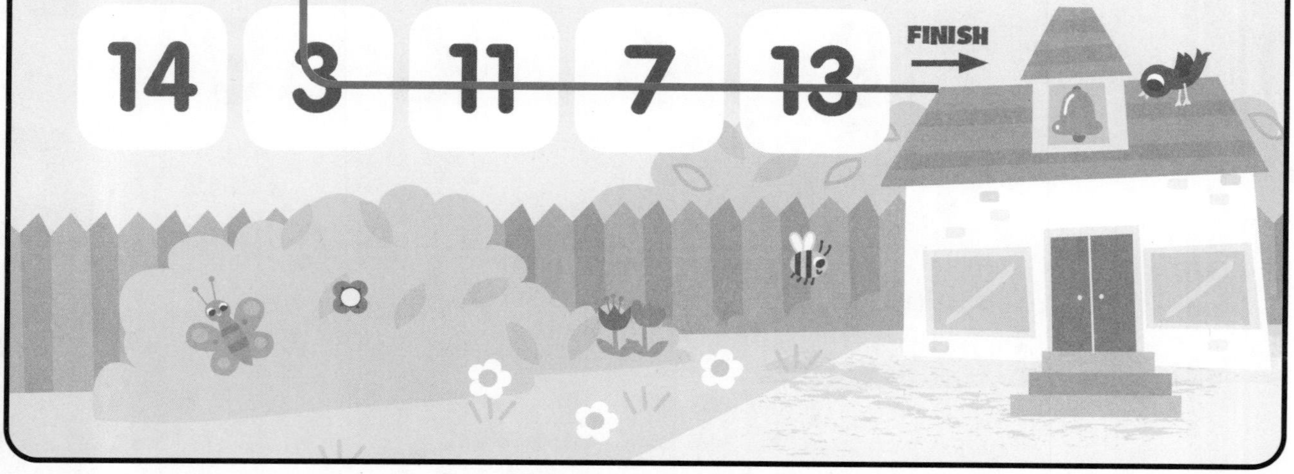

MAZE CRAZE
IT'S EVEN!

Meet Even Steven. Help him find his way to Even Street.
The correct path is made up of only even numbers.
But watch out! The numbers are not in order!
You may not move diagonally.

START

	6	10	9	8	14	6
7	5	2	4	12	13	4
1	3	13	15	11	9	10
5	4	7	6	8	12	2
9	6	1	14	3	7	11
11	7	15	10	4		15

FINISH →

EVEN ST.

ANSWERS

MAZE CRAZE
IT'S EVEN!

Meet Even Steven. Help him find his way to Even Street.
The correct path is made up of only even numbers.
But watch out! The numbers are not in order!
You may not move diagonally.

START

6	10	9	8	14	6	
7	5	2	4	12	13	4
1	3	13	15	11	9	10
5	4	7	6	8	12	2
9	6	1	14	3	7	11
11	7	15	10	4		15

FINISH →

EVEN ST.

LET'S FIND WORDS!

Look at the puzzle and see if you can find each word listed. They all start with the letter **F**! Look for the words across and up and down.

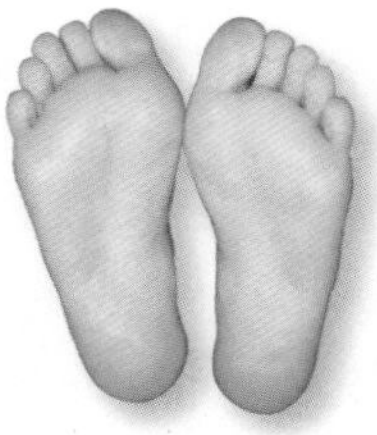

FEET

FOX

FROG

FISH

FEATHER

FAN

F	E	A	T	H	E	R
J	E	O	G	X	F	S
M	J	A	K	N	A	E
E	R	E	A	O	F	F
F	E	E	T	R	O	R
A	I	A	G	E	X	O
N	F	I	S	H	I	G

ANSWERS

LET'S FIND WORDS!

Look at the puzzle and see if you can find each word listed. They all start with the letter **F**! Look for the words across and up and down.

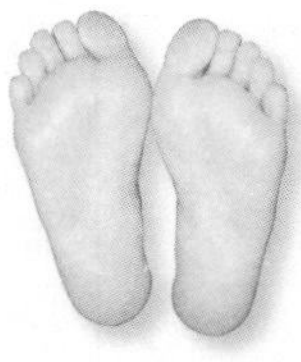

FEET

FOX

FROG

FISH

FEATHER

FAN

F	E	A	T	H	E	R
J	E	O	G	X	F	S
M	J	A	K	N	A	E
E	R	E	A	O	F	F
F	E	E	T	R	O	R
A	I	A	G	E	X	O
N	F	I	S	H	I	G

RIDDLE TIME!

Write the first letter of each object to answer this riddle:

What did the brother tree say to the pesky baby tree?

___ ___ ___ ___

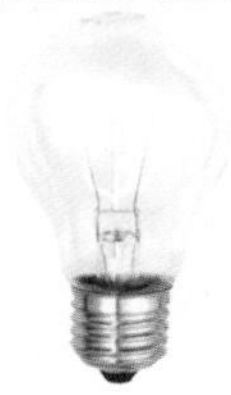   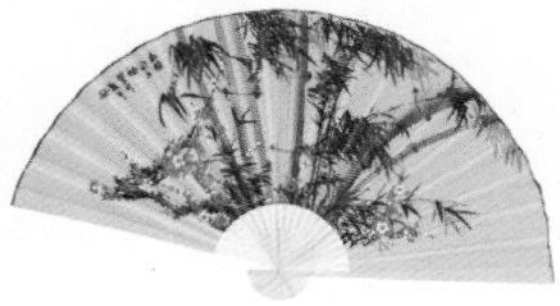

___ ___

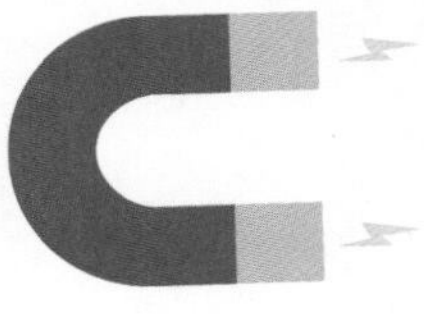 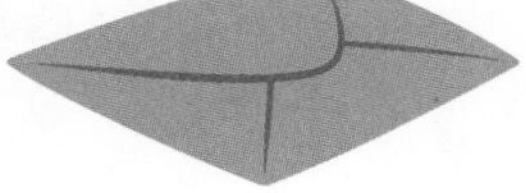

___ ___ ___ ___ ___

Answer: ____________________

ANSWERS

RIDDLE TIME!

Write the first letter of each object to answer this riddle:

What did the brother tree say to the pesky baby tree?

L E A F

M E

A L O N E

Answer: LEAF ME ALONE

FALLING LEAVES

Unscramble the colors of these fall leaves.

DER

____

ANGERO

____

PLEPUR

____

OGDL

____

WNORB

____

WELLYO

____

ANSWERS

FALLING LEAVES

Unscramble the colors of these fall leaves.

DER
RED

ANGERO
ORANGE

PLEPUR
PURPLE

OGDL
GOLD

WNORB
BROWN

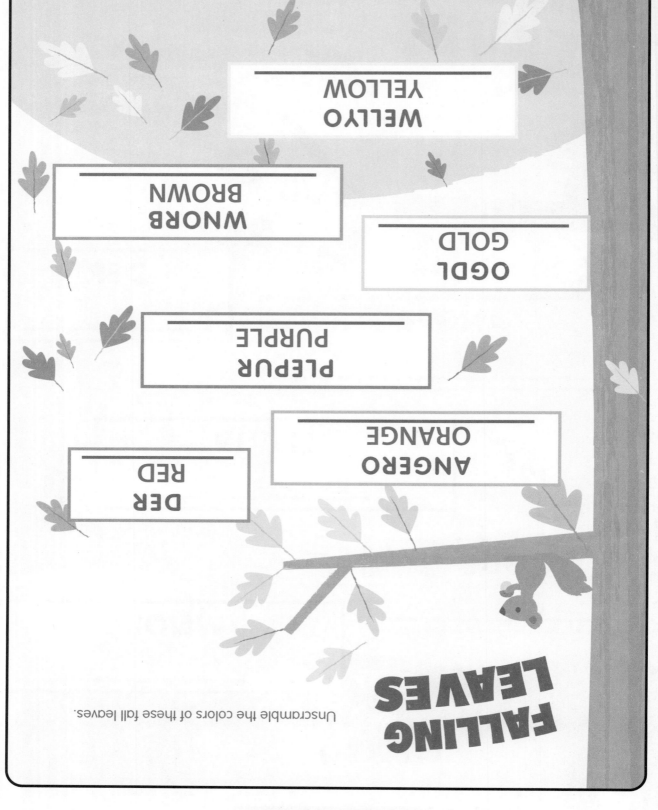

WELLYO
YELLOW

APPLE PICKING

In fall, apples are ripe and ready to pick.
See how many words you can make out of

APPLE PICKING

ANSWERS

APPLE PICKING

In fall, apples are ripe and ready to pick.
See how many words you can make out of

APPLE PICKING

Here are words you might have made:

PIG	PAIN
LEAP	NICE
PAGE	INK
CAGE	LEAK
PECAN	PINK
LICK	CAKE
PAL	PACK

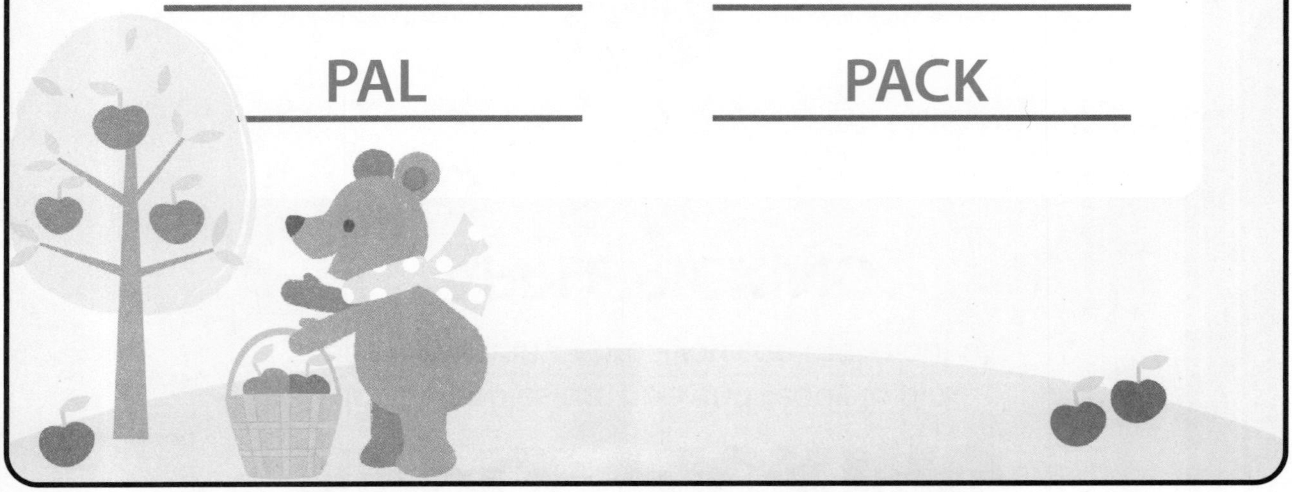

SECRET CODE

Shh! Use this secret code to answer this riddle:

What did one snowman say to the other snowman?

1=V 3=H 5=A 7=I 9=E

2=C 4=D 6=N 8=Y

Answer:

____ ____ ____ ____   ____ ____

3 5 1 9   5 6

____ ____ ____   ____ ____ ____

7 2 9   4 5 8

ANSWERS

SECRET CODE

Shh! Use this secret code to answer this riddle:

What did one snowman say to the other snowman?

1=V	3=H	5=A	7=I	9=E
2=C	4=D	6=N	8=Y	

Answer:

H	A	V	E		A	N
3	5	1	9		5	6

I	C	E		D	A	Y
7	2	9		4	5	8

CAN YOU FIND?

Search, find, and circle these things in the kitchen!

4 cupcakes

1 cake

3 rolls of paper towels

1 bowl

3 spoons

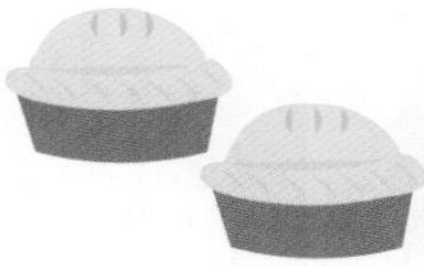

2 pies

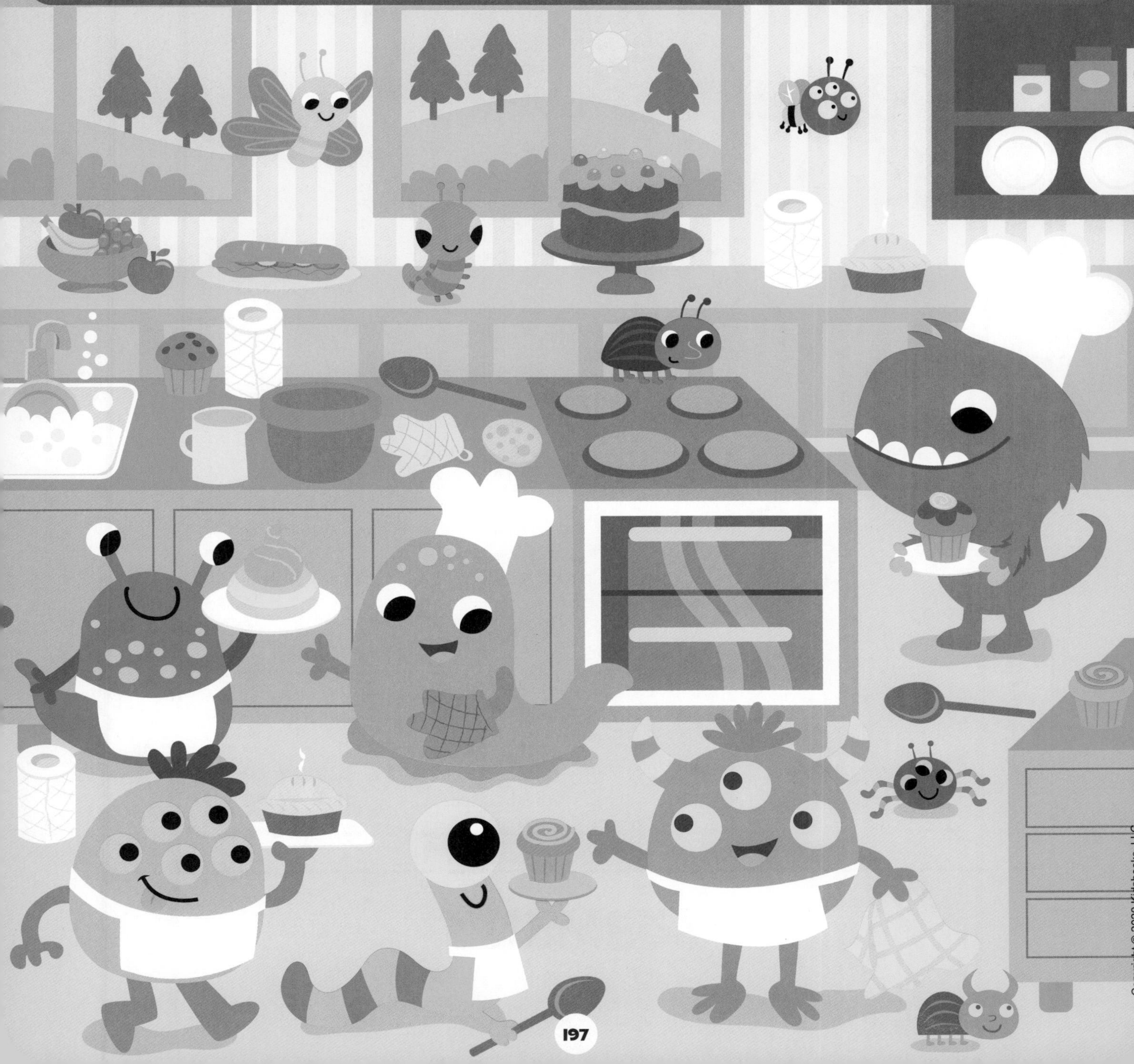

ANSWERS

CAN you FIND?
Search, find, and circle these things in the kitchen!
4 cupcakes
1 cake
3 rolls of paper towels
1 bowl
3 spoons
2 pies

LET'S MAKE WORDS!

Write as many words as you can that start with the letter **B**.
Be creative! See if you can think of five words.

B ____________________

B ____________________

B ____________________

B ____________________

B ____________________

ANSWERS

LET'S MAKE WORDS!

Write as many words as you can that start with the letter **B**.
Be creative! See if you can think of five words.

Here are a few words:

BEAR

BASKET

BALL

BIKE

BLANKET

NAME THE ANIMALS

Use the clues to complete this crossword puzzle. All the animal names start with S.

ACROSS

1. Makes a stink
2. Great white ______________
3. Has five arms

DOWN

1. Spins a web
2. Goes hiss
3. Moves very slowly
4. Lives on land and in water; barks like a dog

1
2
3
4

ANSWERS

NAME THE ANIMALS

Use the clues to complete this crossword puzzle.
All the animal names start with S.

ACROSS

1. Makes a stink
2. Great white
3. Has five arms

DOWN

1. Spins a web
2. Goes hiss
3. Moves very slowly
4. Lives on land and in water; barks like a dog

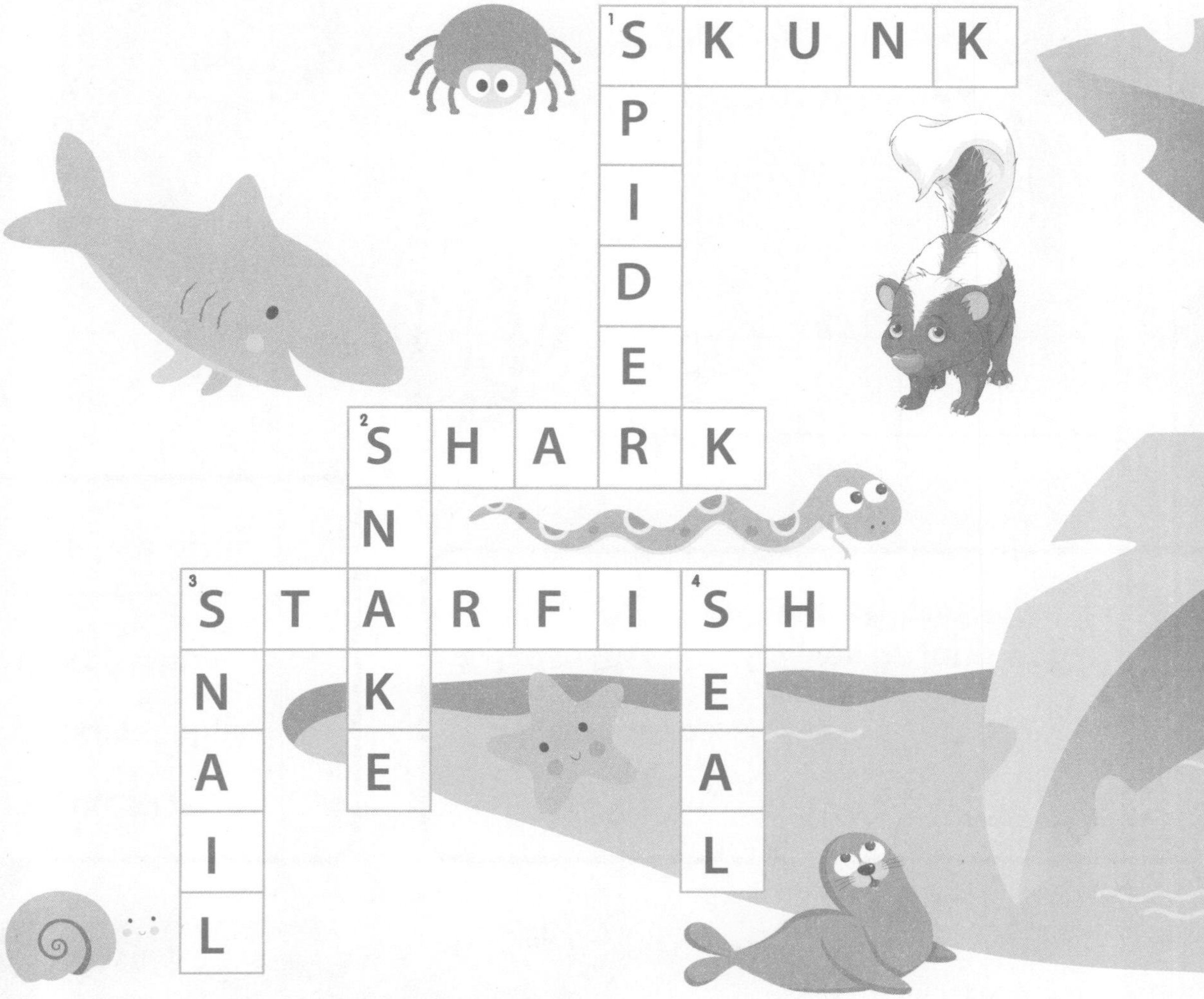
1 SKUNK
SPIDER
2 SHARK
SNAKE
3 STARFISH
SNAIL
4 SEAL

SPOT THE DIFFERENCE ON THE STREET

Circle five things that are different in these two pictures.

ANSWERS

SPOT THE DIFFERENCE ON THE STREET

Circle five things that are different in these two pictures.

NAME TAG RIDDLE

These students all have name tags.
Write the first letter of each name to answer this riddle:

Why was the broom late for school?

Sam

Wendy

Eric

Pam

Tom

ANSWER:

IT OVER-________________________

ANSWERS

NAME TAG RIDDLE

These students all have name tags.
Write the first letter of each name to answer this riddle:

Why was the broom late for school?

Sam
S
Wendy
W
Eric
E
Pam
P
Tom
T

ANSWER:

IT OVER- SWEPT

NAME TAG RIDDLE

These students all have name tags.
Write the first letter of each name to answer this riddle:

Who is the king of school?

Rob
Una
Lisa
Eric
Rick

ANSWER:

THE ______________________________

ANSWERS

NAME TAG RIDDLE

These students all have name tags.
Write the first letter of each name to answer this riddle:

Who is the king of school?

Rob
R
Una
U
Lisa
L
Eric
E
Rick
R

ANSWER:

THE RULER

CAN YOU FIND?

Search, find, and circle these things at a birthday party.

1 crown

6 cupcakes

2 blue gifts

1 soccer ball

4 envelopes

2 party hats

ANSWERS

CAN YOU FIND?
Search, find, and circle
these things at a birthday party.
1 crown
6 cupcakes
2 blue gifts
1 soccer
ball
4 envelopes
2 party hats

WHICH IS DIFFERENT?

Find one butterfly that is different from the rest.

ANSWERS

WHICH IS DIFFERENT?

Find one butterfly that is different from the rest.

REBUS FUN

Solve this rebus puzzle to find out which rescue truck is first to the scene!

 - L + U +

 - DDER +  - FE

_ _ _ _ _ _ _ _ _

Answer:

ANSWERS

REBUS FUN

Solve this rebus puzzle to find out which rescue truck is first to the scene!

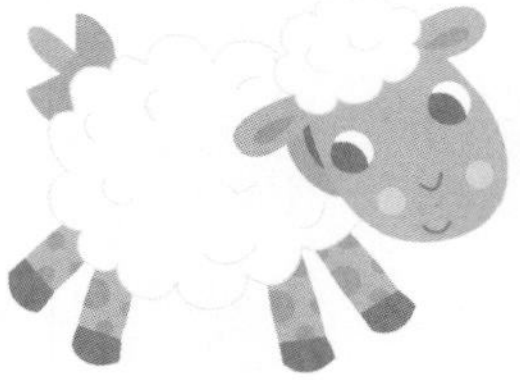 - L + U +

 - DDER +  - FE

A M B U L A N C E

Answer:

AMBULANCE

MAZE CRAZE DIMES!

This girl has saved lots of dimes.
Help her put them in the piggy bank.
The correct path is made up only of dimes.
You may not move diagonally.

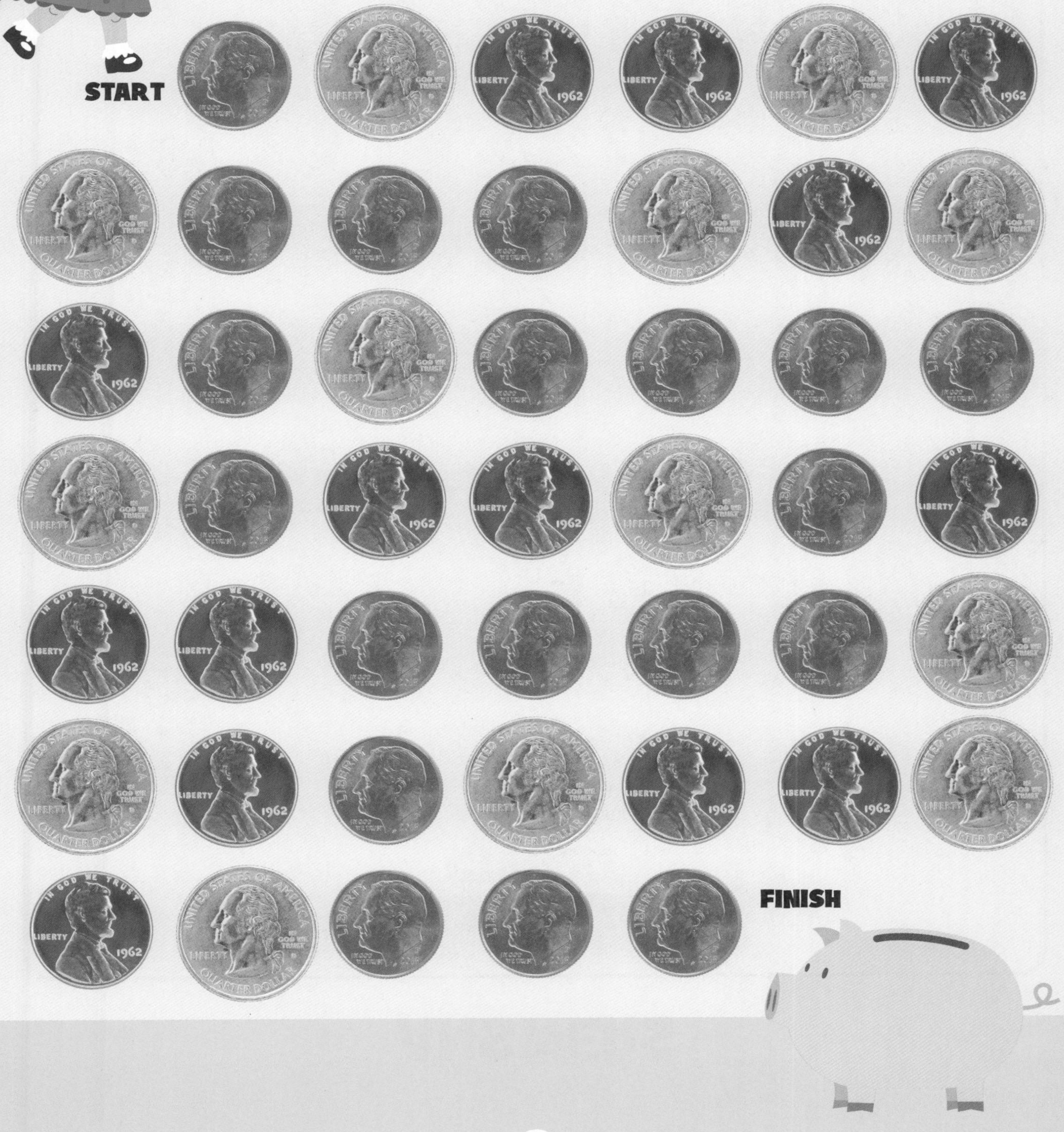
START
FINISH

ANSWERS

MAZE CRAZE DIMES!

This girl has saved lots of dimes.
Help her put them in the piggy bank.
The correct path is made up only of dimes.
You may not move diagonally.

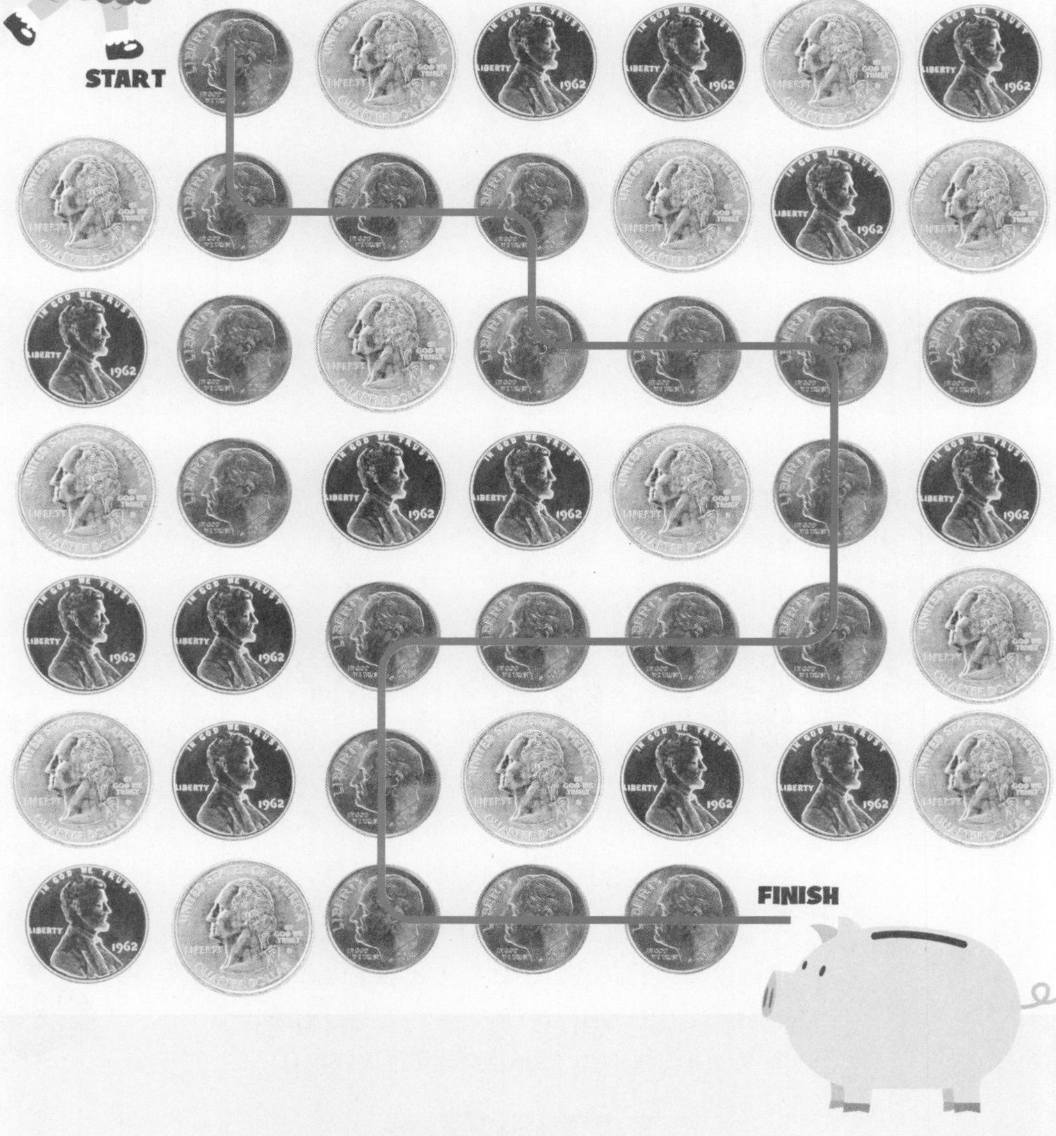
START
FINISH

FILL IT IN!

Fill in the missing letters to read this list of supplies.

___ ANNED FOOD

FL___SHLIGHT

___ATCHES

MA___

KN___FE

SPOO___

SLEEPING BA___

___ENT

FO___K

FIRST AID K___T

BUG S___RAY

Now write those letters in the spaces below and find out why you need everything on the list!

___ ___ ___ ___ ___ ___ ___

___ ___ ___ ___

ANSWERS

FILL IT IN!

Fill in the missing letters to read this list of supplies.

C ANNED FOOD

FL A SHLIGHT

M ATCHES

MA P

KN I FE

SPOO N

SLEEPING BA G

T ENT

FO R K

FIRST AID K I T

BUG S P RAY

Now write those letters in the spaces below and find out why you need everything on the list!

C A M P I N G

T R I P

CAN YOU FIND?

Search, find, and circle these things at the campout.

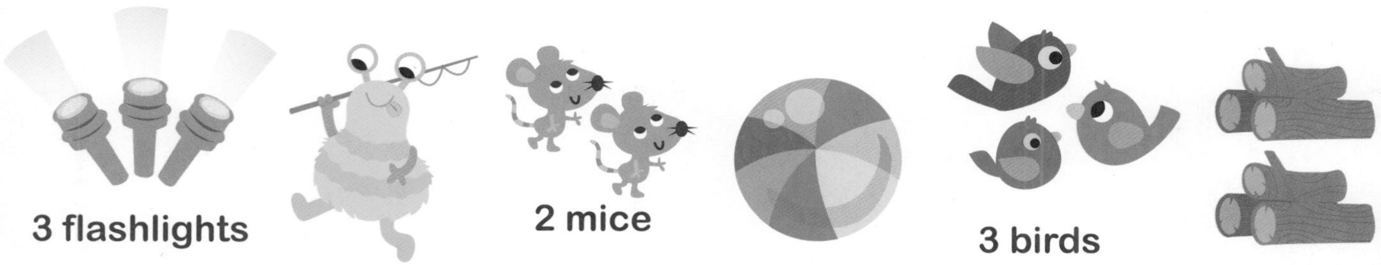

3 flashlights

1 fishing monster

2 mice

1 beach ball

3 birds

2 firewood bundles

ANSWERS

CAN you FIND?

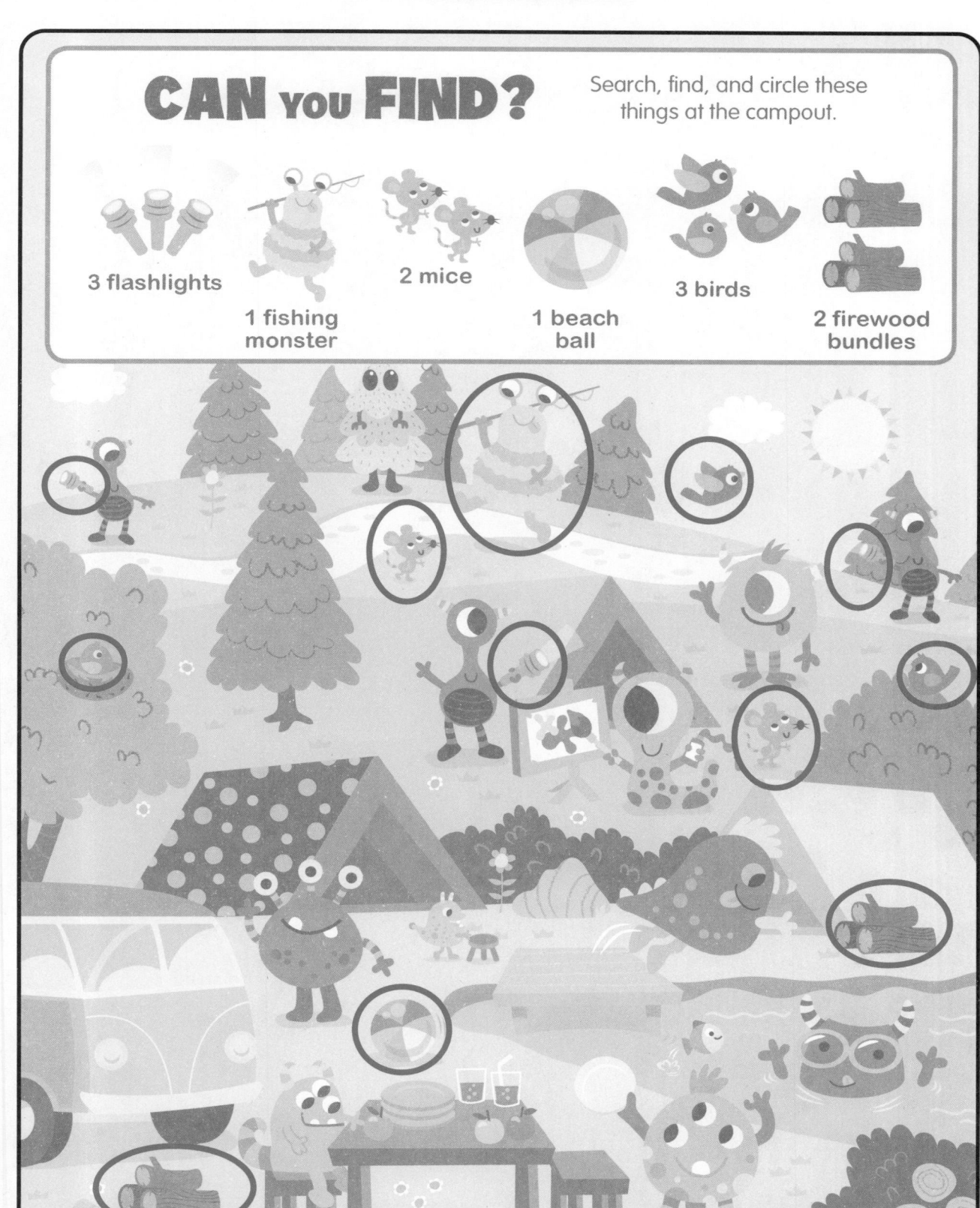

Search, find, and circle these things at the campout.

- 3 flashlights
- 1 fishing monster
- 2 mice
- 1 beach ball
- 3 birds
- 2 firewood bundles

LET'S CIRCLE!

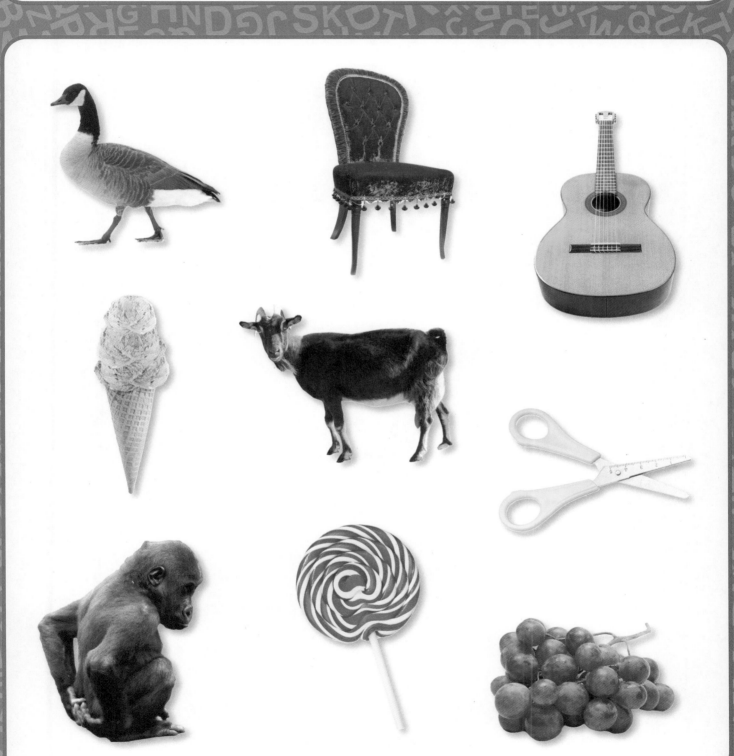

Circle five things that start with the letter **G**.

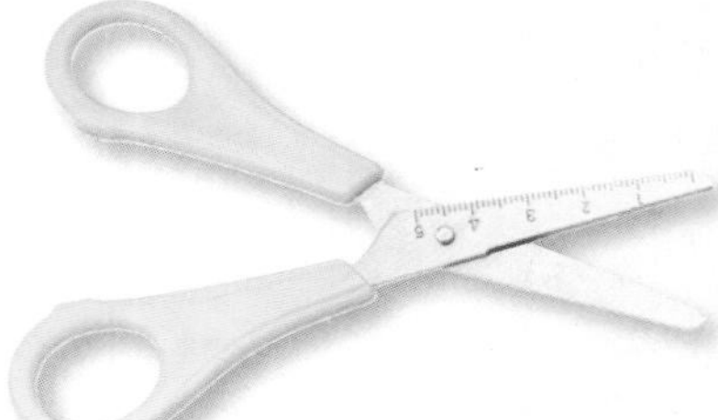

ANSWERS

LET'S CIRCLE!

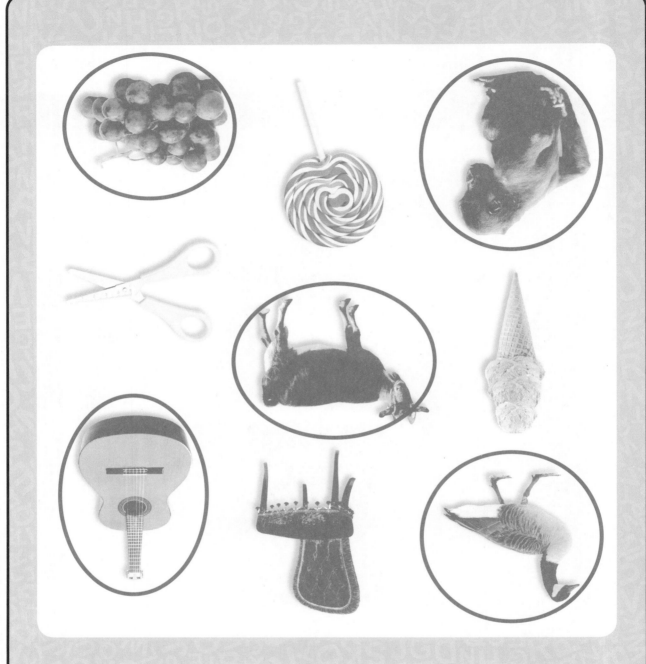

Circle five things that start with the letter **G**.

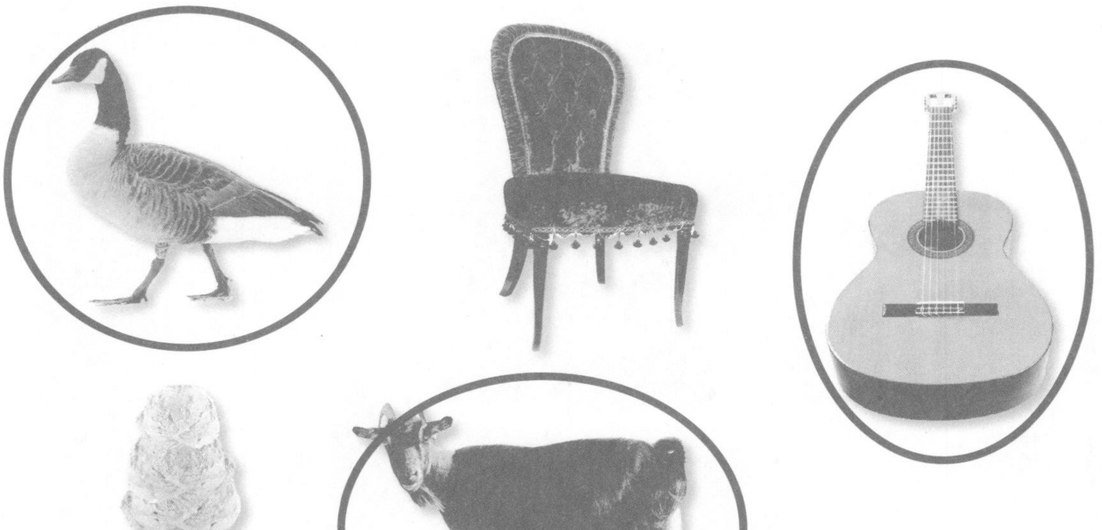

FIX 'N' MATCH

Unscramble the words.
Then match each one with its rhyme.

KCUD ____________

LLAF ____________

LCKOC ____________

ERET ____________

RIWE ____________

ANSWERS

FIX 'N' MATCH

Unscramble the words.
Then match each one with its rhyme.

KCUD DUCK

LLAF FALL

LCKOC CLOCK

ERET TREE

RIWE WIRE

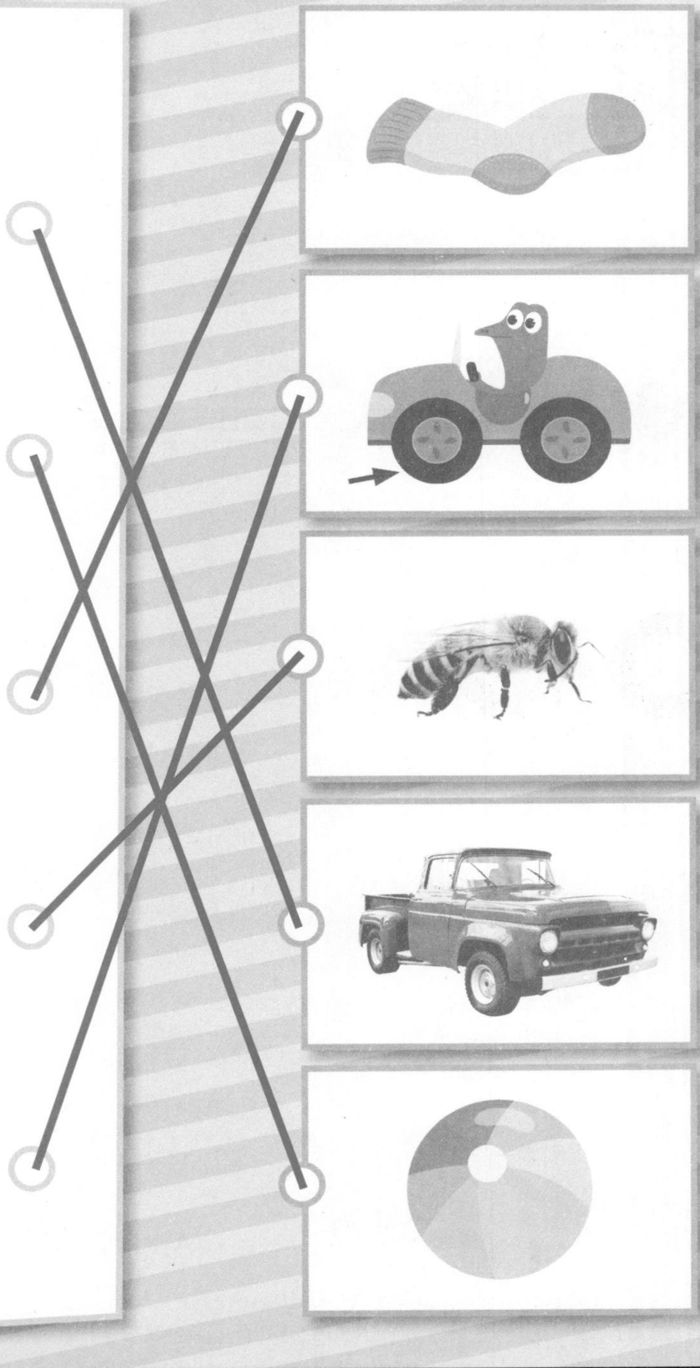

DOT TO DOT

Who is catching the ball?
Connect the dots from 1 to 25 and find out.

1
2
3
4
5
6
7
8
9
10
11
12
13
14
15
16
17
18
19
20
21
22
23
24
25

ANSWERS

DOT TO DOT

Who is catching the ball?
Connect the dots from 1 to 25 and find out.

1
2
3
4
5
6
7
8
9
10
11
12
13
14
15
16
17
18
19
20
21
22
23
24
25

IT'S MAGIC!

Try this magic trick:
Turn a CAKE into a MAZE.

You don't need a magic wand.
Just change one letter at a time.

CAKE

CA ___ E

___ A ___ E

___ A ___ E

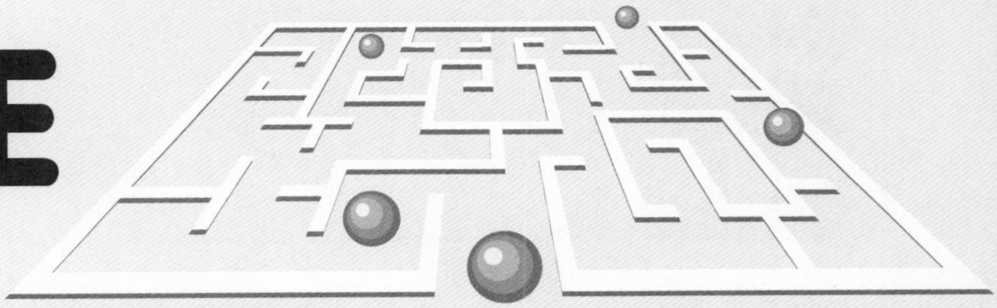

ANSWERS

IT'S MAGIC!

Try this magic trick:
Turn a CAKE into a MAZE.

You don't need a magic wand.
Just change one letter at a time.

CAKE

CA<u>N</u>E

<u>M</u>A<u>N</u>E

<u>M</u>A<u>Z</u>E

SPOT THE DIFFERENCE AT THE HARBOR

Circle five things that are different in these two pictures.

ANSWERS

SPOT THE DIFFERENCE AT THE HARBOR

Circle five things that are different in these two pictures.

WHICH IS DIFFERENT?

Find one robot that is different from the rest.

ANSWERS

WHICH is DIFFERENT?

Find one robot that is different from the rest.

REBUS FUN

Solve the rebus puzzle to answer this question:

What do you call a dog that likes bubble baths?

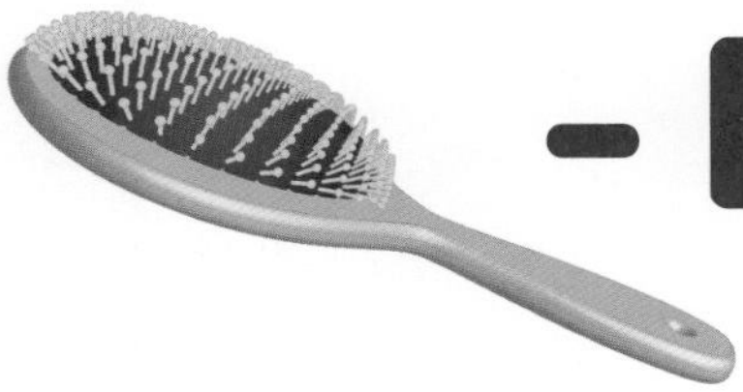 - BRU +  - L

____ ____ ____ ____ ____ -

 - B - K +  - PUD

____ ____ ____ ____ ____

Answer:

__________ - ____________

ANSWERS

REBUS FUN

Solve the rebus puzzle to answer this question:

What do you call a dog that likes bubble baths?

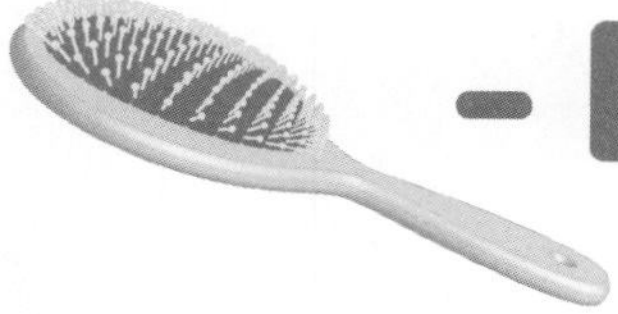 - BRU +  - L

S H A M P -

 - B - K +  - PUD

O O D L E

Answer:

SHAMP - OODLE

MAZE CRAZE PUPPY!

Help this puppy find its mother.
The correct path is made up only of paw prints.
You may not move diagonally.

START
FINISH

ANSWERS

MAZE CRAZE PUPPY!

Help this puppy find its mother.
The correct path is made up only of paw prints.
You may not move diagonally.

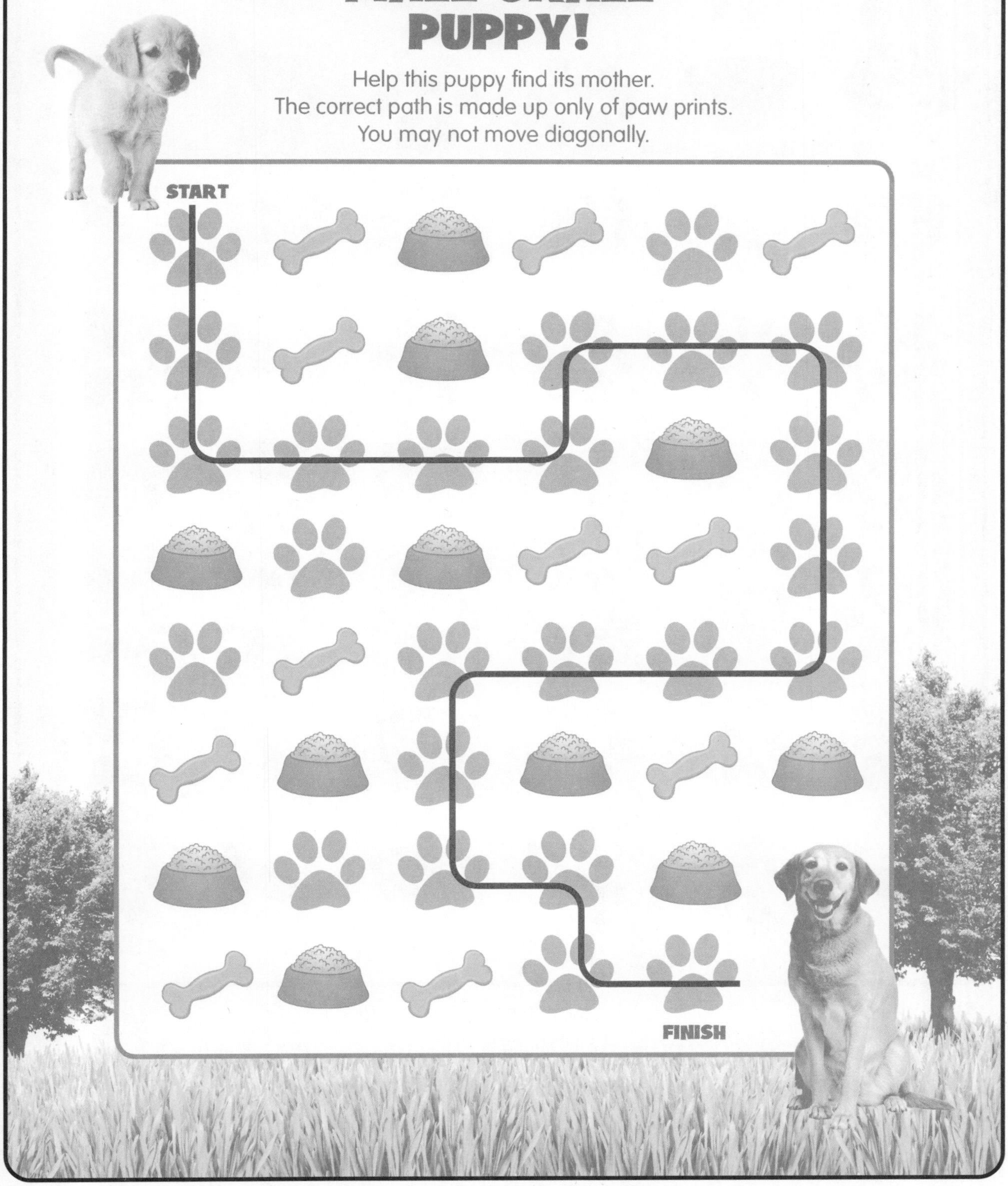
START
FINISH

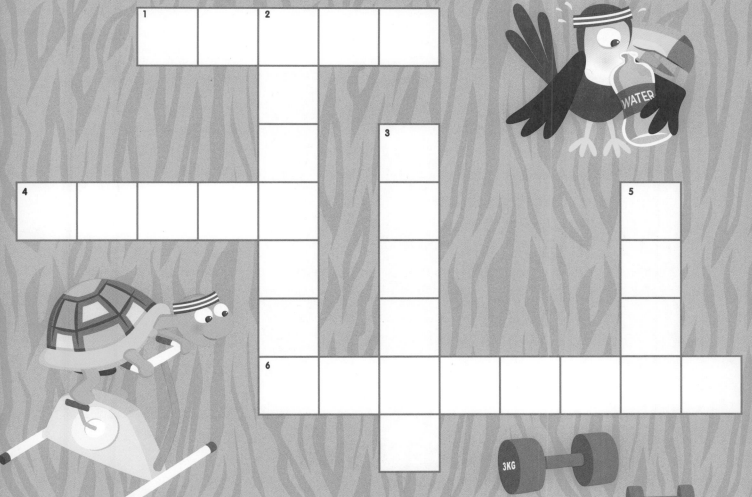

NAME THE WILD ANIMALS AT THE GYM!

Use the picture clues to complete this crossword puzzle.

ACROSS

1. 

4. 

6. 

DOWN

2. 

3. 

5. 

WATER

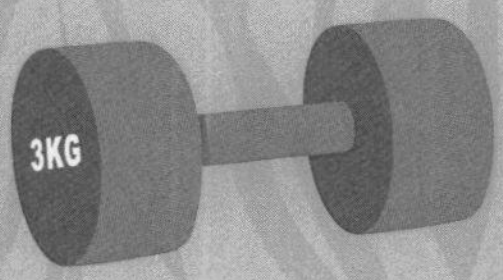
3KG

ANSWERS

NAME THE WILD ANIMALS AT THE GYM!

Use the picture clues to complete this crossword puzzle.

ACROSS

1. 4. 6.

DOWN

2. 3. 5.

1 Across: TIGER
4 Across: ZEBRA
6 Across: ELEPHANT

2 Down: GIRAFFE
3 Down: MONKEY
5 Down: LION

WATER

SECRET CODE

Shh! Use this secret code to answer this riddle:

What goes up, but never comes down?

1=U 3=O 5=G 7=E

2=A 4=R 6=Y

Answer:

___ ___ ___ ___

6 3 1 4

___ ___ ___

2 5 7

ANSWERS

SECRET CODE

Shh! Use this secret code to answer this riddle:

What goes up, but never comes down?

1=U 3=O 5=G 7=E

2=A 4=R 6=Y

Answer:

Y O U R

6 3 1 4

A G E

2 5 7

LOOK-ALIKES

Which two silly monsters are exactly the same?

ANSWERS

LOOK-ALIKES

Which two silly monsters are exactly the same?

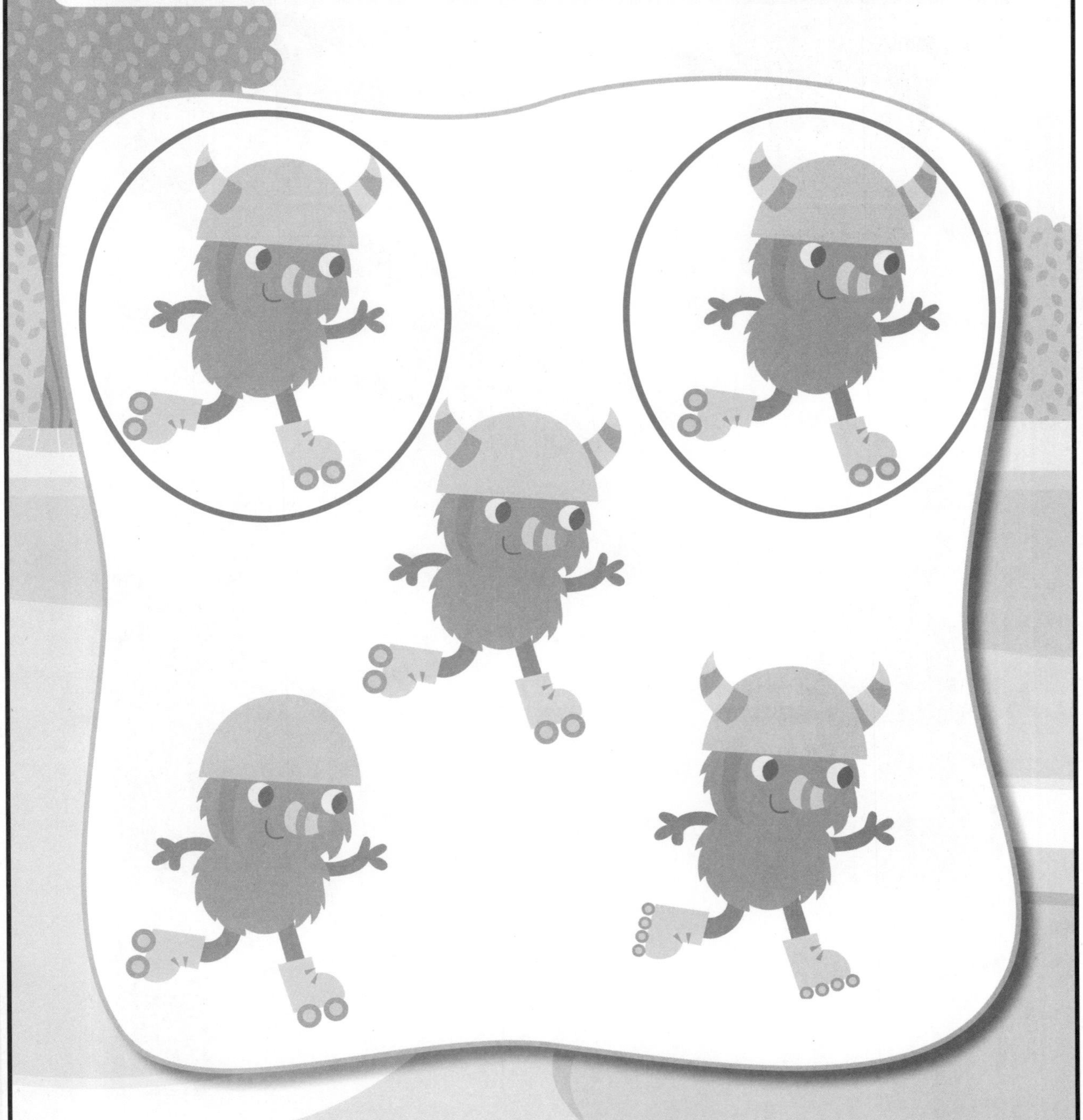

LET'S MAKE WORDS!

Write as many words as you can that start with the letter **K**.
Be creative! See if you can think of five words.

K ______________________

K ______________________

K ______________________

K ______________________

K ______________________

ANSWERS

LET'S MAKE WORDS!

Write as many words as you can that start with the letter **K**.
Be creative! See if you can think of five words.

Here are a few words:

KANGAROO

KITE

KETTLE

KITTEN

KING

WHAT DOESN'T BELONG?

Circle one thing you would **NOT** find in a grocery store.

ANSWERS

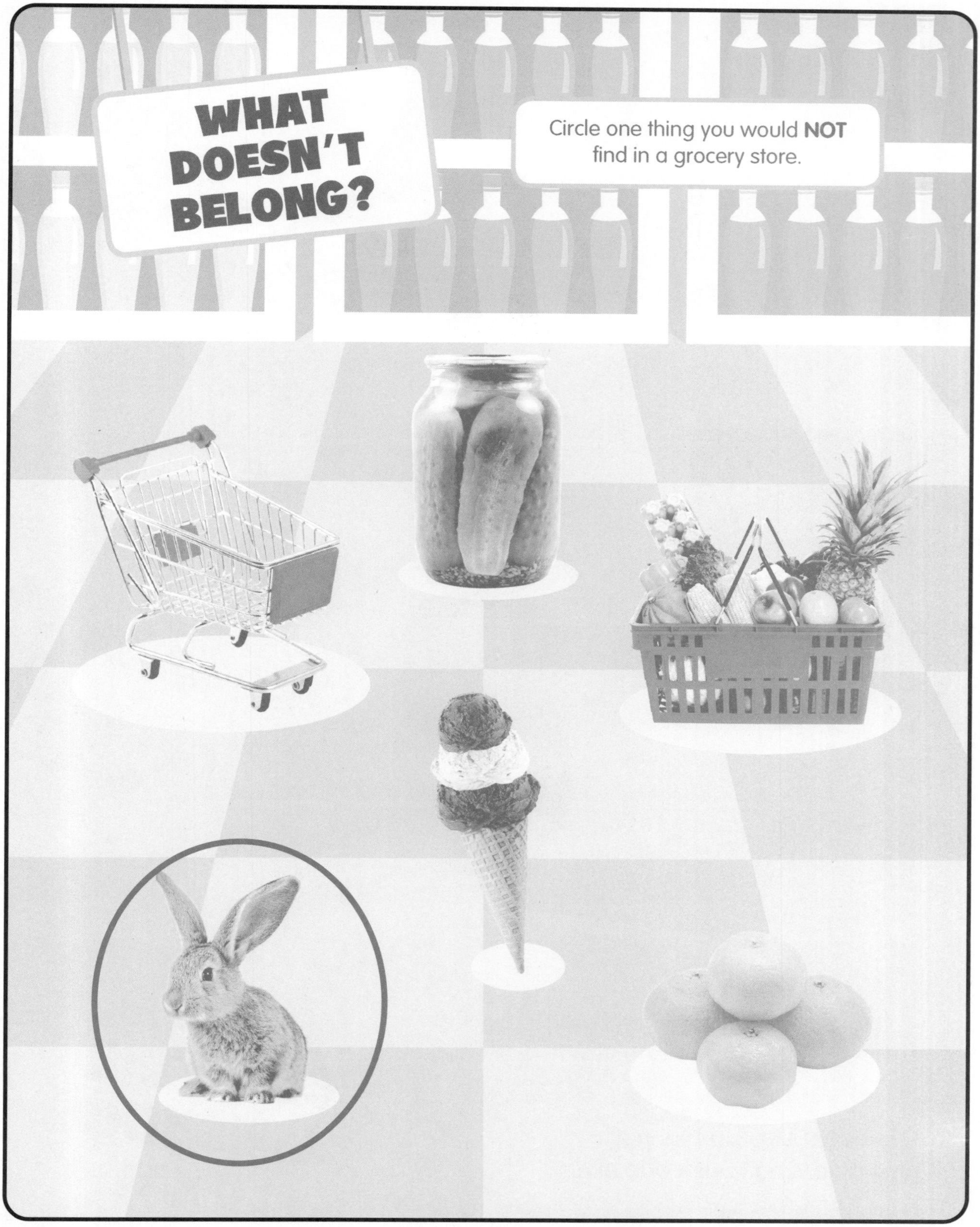
WHAT DOESN'T BELONG?
Circle one thing you would **NOT** find in a grocery store.

GET TO WORK!

Match the pictures that go together.

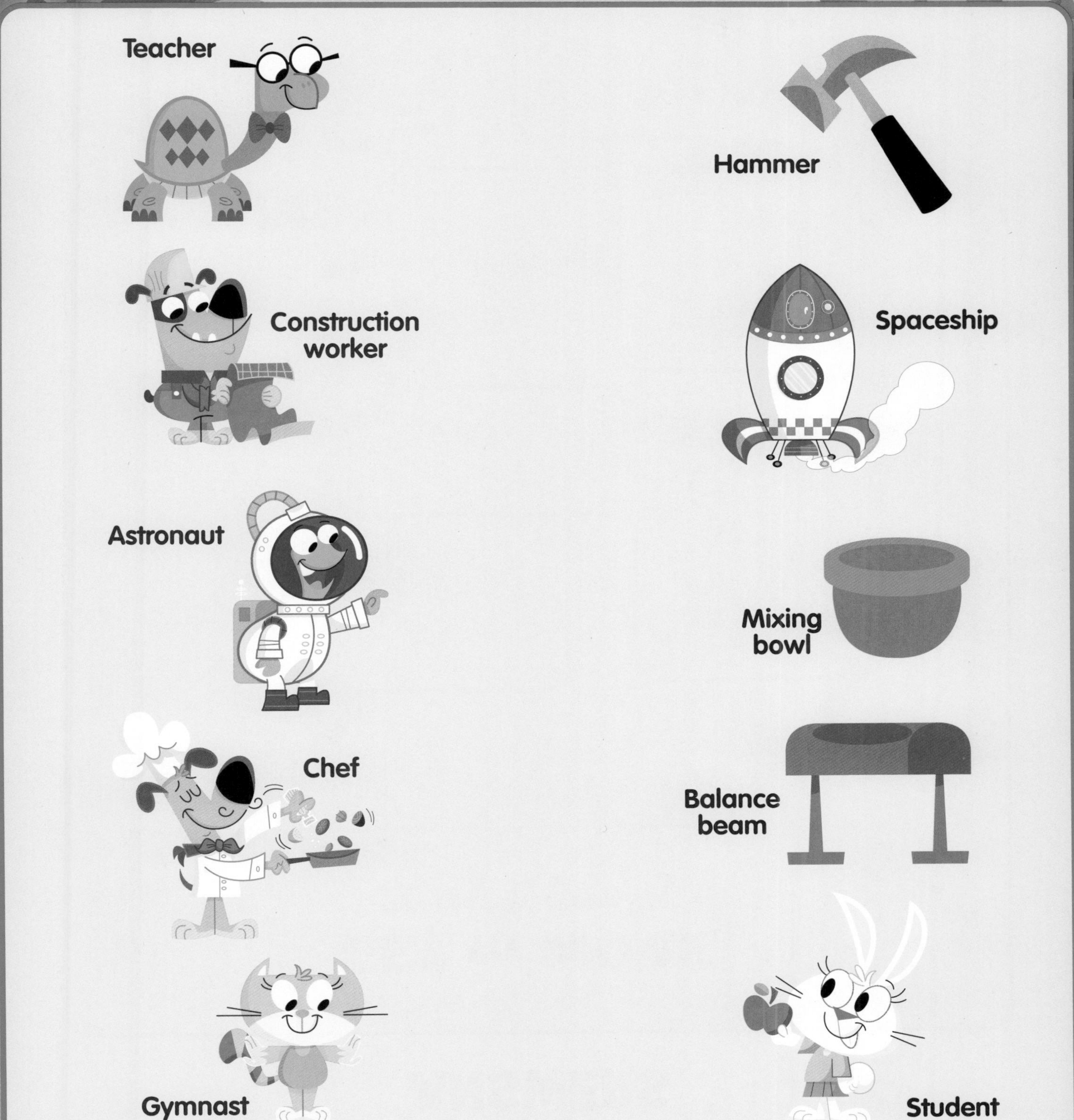
Teacher
Hammer
Construction worker
Spaceship
Astronaut
Mixing bowl
Chef
Balance beam
Gymnast
Student

ANSWERS

GET TO WORK!

Match the pictures that go together.

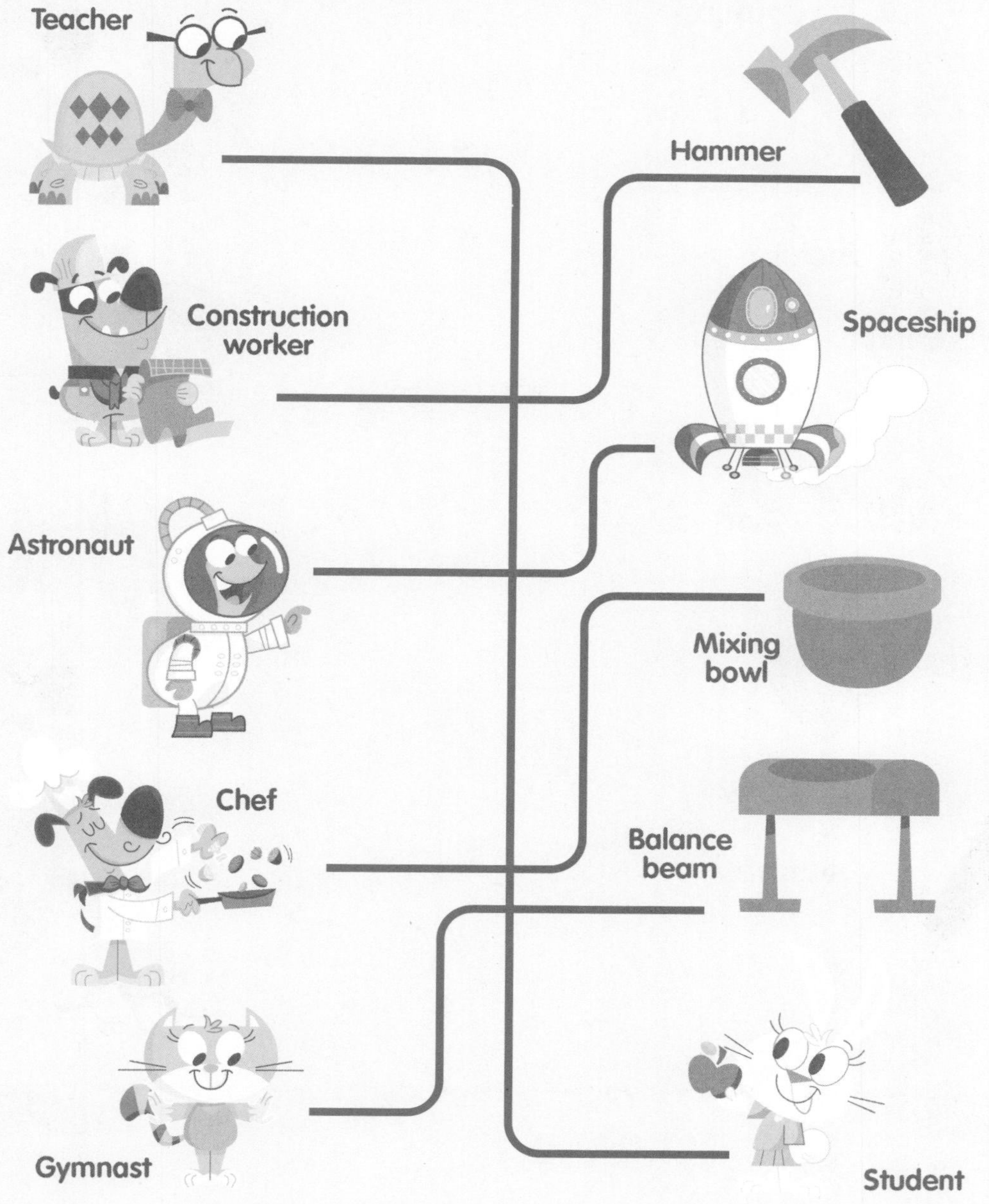
Teacher
Construction worker
Astronaut
Chef
Gymnast
Hammer
Spaceship
Mixing bowl
Balance beam
Student

RIDDLE TIME!

Write the first letter of each object to answer this riddle:

What gets more wet the more it dries?

____

________ ________ ________ ________ ________

567547
TICKET
567547

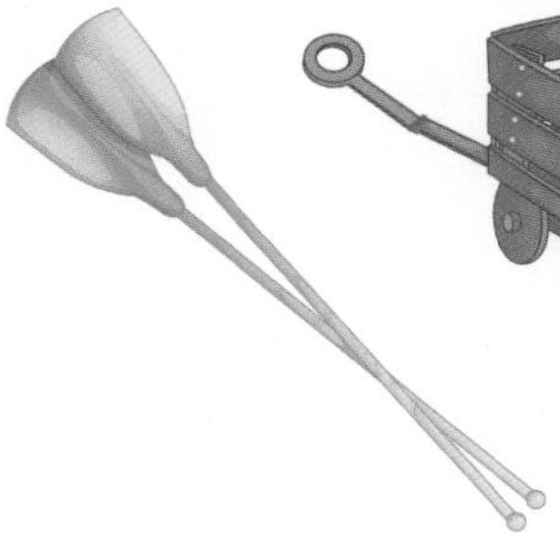

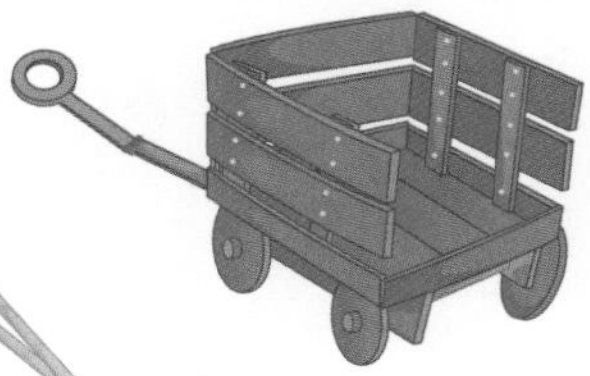

Answer:

____

ANSWERS

RIDDLE TIME!

Write the first letter of each object to answer this riddle:

What gets more wet the more it dries?

A

T O W E L

567547
TICKET
567547

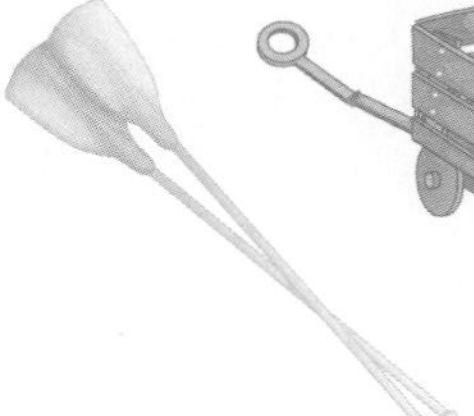

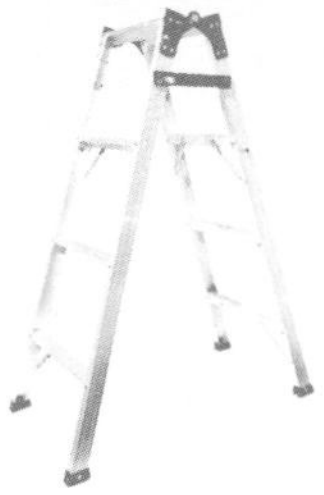

Answer:

A TOWEL

REBUS FUN

Solve the rebus puzzle to answer this question:

What is the longest river in the world?

 - RE ___ ___ ___

 - A + E ___ ___ ___ ___

R +  - D

___ ___ ___ ___ ___

Answer:

____

ANSWERS

REBUS FUN

Solve the rebus puzzle to answer this question:

What is the longest river in the world?

- RE T H E

- A + E N I L E

R +  - D

R I V E R

Answer:

THE NILE RIVER

SNAKE TWINS

Draw a line to connect each snake on the left to its exact twin on the right.

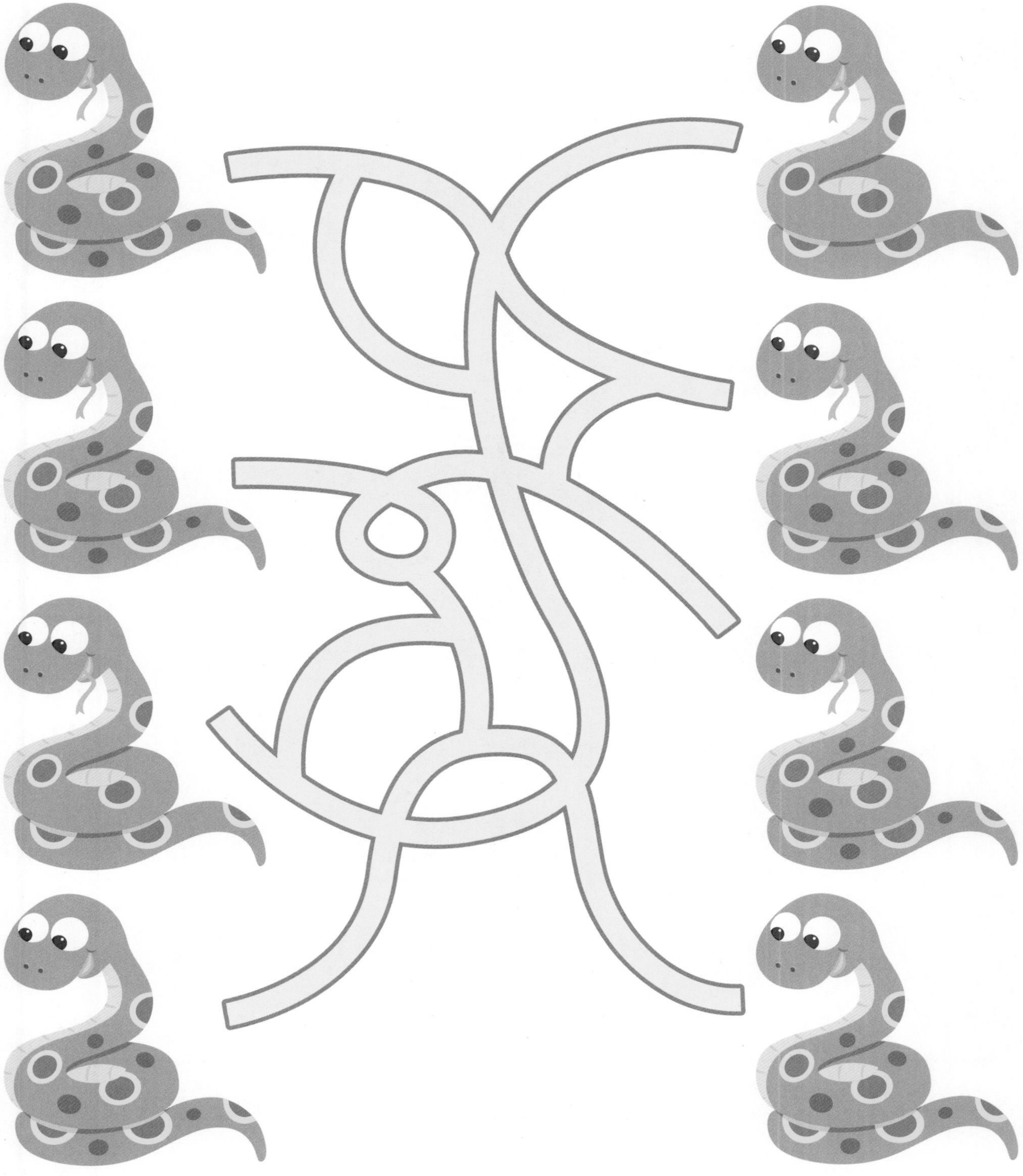

ANSWERS

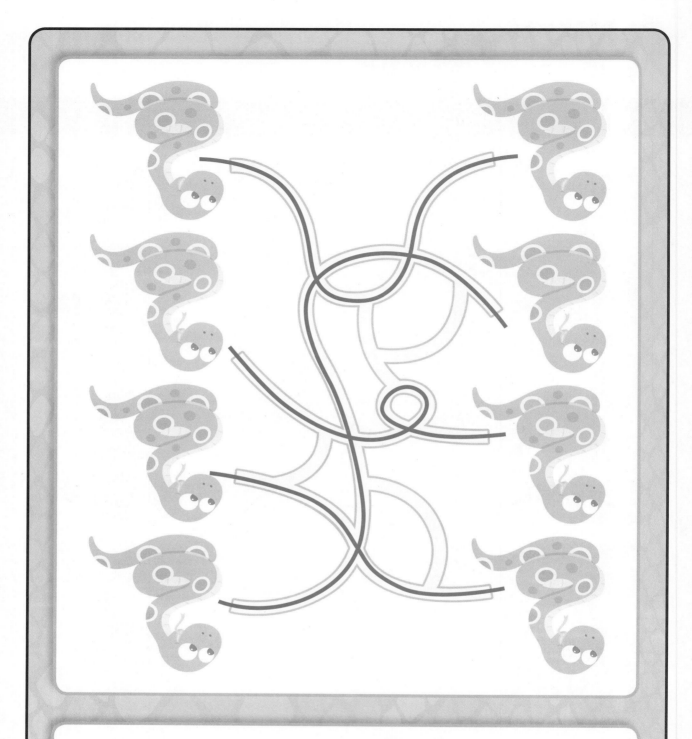

SNAKE TWINS

Draw a line to connect each snake on the left to its exact twin on the right.

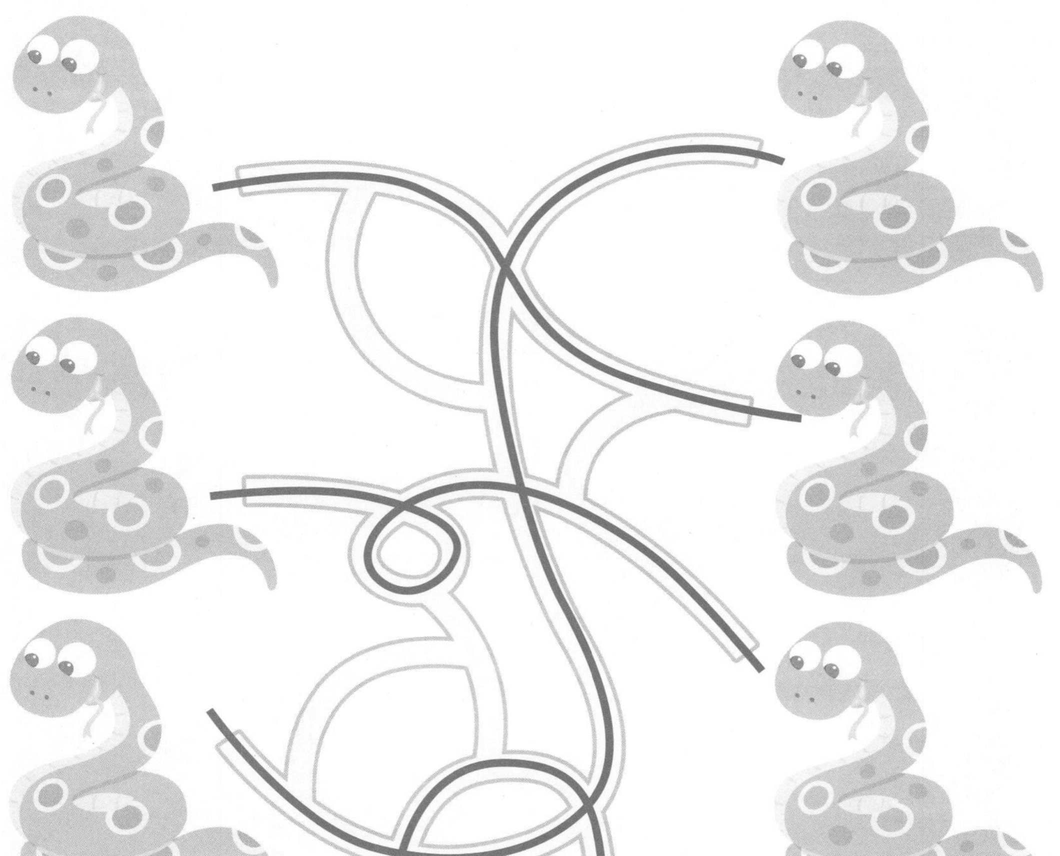

SPOT THE DIFFERENCE AT THE RACE

Circle five things that are different in these two pictures.

ANSWERS

SPOT THE DIFFERENCE AT THE RACE

Circle five things that are different in these two pictures.